KANSAS BOY

Kansas Boy

THE MEMOIR OF A. J. BOLINGER

A. J. Bolinger

EDITED BY
Jeffrey H. Barker and
Melissa Walker

University Press of Kansas

Published by the University Press of Kansas (Lawrence, Kansas 66045), which was organized by the Kansas Board of Regents and is operated and funded by Emporia State University, Fort Hays State University, Kansas State University, Pittsburg State University, the University of Kansas, and Wichita State University.

Library of Congress Cataloging-in-Publication Data
Names: Bolinger, A. J. (Arthur Joel), 1881–1977 author. | Barker, Jeffrey H., 1957– editor. | Walker, Melissa, editor.
Title: Kansas boy : the memoir of A. J. Bolinger / by A. J. Bolinger ; edited by Jeffrey H. Barker and Melissa Walker.
Description: [Lawrence, Kansas] : University Press of Kansas, [2021]
Identifiers: LCCN 2020036204
ISBN 9780700631858 (cloth)
ISBN 9780700630622 (paperback)
ISBN 9780700630639 (ebook)
Subjects: LCSH: Bolinger, A. J. (Arthur Joel), 1881–1977. | Judges—United States—Biography. | Lawyers—United States—Biography.
Classification: LCC KF8745.B59 B65 2021 | DDC 347.778/0234 [B]—dc23
LC record available at https://lccn.loc.gov/2020036204.

British Library Cataloguing-in-Publication Data is available.

Printed in the United States of America

10 9 8 7 6 5 4 3 2 1

The paper used in this publication is acid free and meets the minimum requirements of the American National Standard for Permanence of Paper for Printed Library Materials Z39.48-1992.

Contents

~

Acknowledgments

We are grateful to several people whose assistance and encouragement helped bring this book to life.

Jeff Barker acknowledges the materials and assistance from the several branches of the Bolinger family, especially from A. J.'s grandchildren, my cousins: Dwight Bolinger's son Bruce, William Bolinger Sr.'s son, William Jr., and Mary Concannon, daughter of Margaret Ruth Bolinger McKinley.

This book would not have been possible without the extensive support and encouragement of A. J.'s fourth and youngest child, my late mother, Mary Julia Bolinger Barker.

And then there's A. J.: a larger-than-life figure in my childhood, and to this day. He guided all of his children and grandchildren in so many ways.

A. J. Bolinger's original manuscript was typed on legal-size paper. Converse College graduate Madison Boyd Clarke, then the student assistant in the history and politics department, devoted many hours to entering the manuscript into Microsoft Word files. We appreciate her efforts.

We completed this manuscript in 2008, just as the world economy crashed. University presses were facing severe budget cuts, and we were unable to find a publisher who could take on this book. Fast forward to 2019 when Melissa Walker mentioned the manuscript to historian William Allison. He was intrigued with her description of the memoir and urged her to submit it to University Press of Kansas. We are grateful that he nudged us to persist with the project and helped us navigate the submission process at the Press.

We are also grateful to the staff at University Press of Kansas for their support.

Introduction

On October 27, 1967, retired lawyer and judge Arthur Joel (A. J.) Bolinger (1881–1977) wrote to his son Dwight, "I mailed the mss. yesterday. Edit it all you want. Cut out anything you think improper and if you have time see if you can peddle it. I'm not at all sure whether it is any good or not."[1] The manuscript to which he referred was an account of his youth in Kansas and his young adulthood in Oklahoma. At the urging of his children, the octogenarian had finally set to paper his recollections of these tumultuous years. Although there is no evidence in the family records that Dwight ever "peddled" the manuscript, copies were passed down to descendants. Dwight's copy of the manuscript and supporting materials remained with him in California until his death in 1992 and then passed to his son Bruce, who retains the materials. The original typescript remained in the family home in Versailles, Morgan County, Missouri, in the care of A. J.'s son, William Harrison Bolinger, who had followed his father into the law, serving (also following A. J.) as an attorney and judge in Morgan County.[2] When William's son—also William Bolinger—opened his father's safe deposit box upon his father's death in 2005, the original typescript emerged, nearly forty years after it was written.

From there, a copy was sent to A. J.'s daughter, Mary J. Barker, who passed it to the editors, including her son (A. J.'s grandson), Jeffrey H. Barker. That copy and related materials have been compared with materials held by Bruce Bolinger in the preparation of this book. The resulting memoir is a compilation of the William and Bruce Bolinger materials, with the majority of the memoir emerging from the original typewritten manuscript found by William Bolinger.

Bolinger's memoir offers the twenty-first-century reader delightful and revealing insights on life at a transitional moment in American history. He describes those years as "bursting with energy, wild with ambition." The nation had survived the violent cataclysm of the Civil War and was proceeding with the business of subduing its territory from sea to sea. Anything seemed possible. In many areas, such as the Kansas of A. J.'s childhood, frontier settlements were in the process of becoming established communities. Change was a constant. The energy and ambition that A. J. mentioned are apparent on every page of his recollections. He opens his account with a vividly detailed description of the prairie itself, a land of rolling hills where the bluestem grass "was so rich in sugar that it was possible to produce cattle ready for market just by a summer's grazing." He recounts cattle drives and ranching, farming and small-town life. A. J.'s adventurous father liked to take his family on camping trips, and in the process, he exposed his children to a wider world. They enjoyed the hospitality of a family of poor strangers who sheltered the Bolingers from a violent Kansas storm, and they witnessed one of the Oklahoma land rushes. A. J. retells some of frontier Kansas's legends—and debunks more than a few frontier myths.

Part of the memoir's value to the modern reader lies in its revelations of the way one ordinary middle American experienced national events such as presidential election campaigns and the Spanish-American War. The college student A. J. helps temperance activist Carry Nation wage her anti-saloon campaign. He comments on the Populist political ferment that grew out of the agricultural crisis of the 1880s and 1890s. His memoir also illuminates elements of Kansas history. For example, he shows us how agricultural depression could devastate small-town merchants as well as farmers. His family's trajectory demonstrates the way educational aspirations could shape geographic mobility as well as the ways that unpopular political activism could thwart an individual's economic opportunities. Finally, his recollections offer richer texture to our understanding of life at a particular time and place. In this case, Bolinger offers us a deeper understanding of the impact of the nineteenth-century rural and small-town Kansas environment on childhood experiences and adult attitudes.[3]

But Bolinger is more than a chronicler. He is also a philosopher. He filters his interpretations of his early years through the lens of a lifetime of experience as a small-town lawyer, judge, and Republican politician. The memoir is by turns startlingly progressive and deeply conservative. Some of his views seem awfully modern for a man writing in 1967. He dismissed the portrayals of the "old wild West" from "dime novels, the horse operas, and the TV writers" as fictional distortions, maintaining that the real violence of the West was less romantic and far more insidious in its danger than Hollywood would have us believe. He critiques the modern sporting rodeo as "the illegitimate offspring" of the process of breaking saddle horses. He criticizes federal and state governments and white settlers alike for their treatment of Native Americans. Yet A. J. Bolinger is also deeply critical of a generation of young women who wear short skirts and "make themselves playthings" instead of behaving decorously toward the opposite sex. In short, he is the complex mix of wise social commentator and old-fashioned curmudgeon that many of us become as we age. His keen insights and thoughtful commentary offer today's reader a richer understanding of the experiences of life on the prairies and plains.

Bolinger's description of the late nineteenth century as "bursting with energy" was particularly apt. Contemporary observers made similar comments. John Ingalls, a prominent Republican leader during the Kansas territorial period, once wrote that the history of Kansas "is written in capitals. It is punctuated with exclamation points. Its verbs are imperative. Its adjectives are superlative. . . . The aspiration of Kansas is to reach the unattainable." Kansas was a place where investors pursued fortunes as town developers, settlers sought to establish prosperous farms and ranches, and reformers tried to create an ideal society. Other observers of the time agreed.

In 1887, the *New York Times* called Kansas "the great experimental ground of the nation."[4]

Yet Kansas had not always seemed so promising. From Spanish explorer Francisco Vasquez de Coronado's forays into the region in the 1540s, well into the first half of the nineteenth century, most Europeans and Americans saw Kansas as little more than a road to places further west and a home for Indians. Whites commonly perceived the region to be part of "the great American desert," a place too dry and barren to support settlement. Starting in 1821, thousands of men, freight trains, and cattle routinely traversed Kansas via the Santa Fe Trail, the commercial highway stretching from Independence, Missouri, southwestward to Santa Fe. Later in the nineteenth century, cattle were also driven along the Chisholm Trail, which stretched from southern Texas north to the terminus of the Kansas Pacific Railway in Abilene, Kansas, passing within fifteen miles of A. J.'s Elk County home. In Abilene, the livestock were sold and shipped northward and eastward, a practice that continued until the use of barbed wire fencing eliminated the open range and made great overland cattle drives impossible.[5]

Considering the area unfit for white settlement, in the 1830s, the federal government designated much of the territory that would become Kansas as a permanent home for Native Americans. The Osage and Kansas tribes native to the area as well as some northern and eastern tribes were given reservations in the region while southeastern tribes were being resettled further south to Oklahoma. Gradually, the US Army constructed a network of forts in the region, starting with Fort Leavenworth on the Mississippi River in 1827. Well into the middle of the century, the only whites in Kansas were soldiers, missionaries, traders, Indian agents, and people passing through.

The end of the Mexican War and the acquisition of new territory in the Southwest transformed the national perception of Kansas. The territory once on the periphery of American settlement was now at the center of the continental United States. At the same time, railroad technology connected East and West, and based on experiences in states farther north, many Americans realized that the prairie *could* be farmed. Soon Kansas also became the center of the debate over the extension of slavery into the territories. The

1854 Kansas-Nebraska Act organized two new territories and allowed them to decide their slaveholding status on the basis of popular sovereignty—that is, the settlers of each territory would vote on whether to outlaw slavery.[6]

Soon pro- and antislavery settlers—nearly one hundred thousand between 1854 and 1860—flooded Kansas, the southernmost of the two new territories. Free-Soilers and proslavery men grappled for political control of the state. Political wrangling soon gave way to outright violence, as pro- and antislavery forces engaged in guerrilla fighting, burning towns and killing opponents, most famously at Pottawatomie where radical abolitionist John Brown and his supporters ambushed sleeping proslavery settlers and hacked them to death with cutlasses. Ultimately, territorial leaders drafted four different constitutions before the US Congress finally granted the territory its statehood under an antislavery document in 1861. Kansas remained a battleground during the Civil War, plagued by guerrilla fighting and Confederate raiders.[7]

After the war ended, railroad building took hold in earnest in Kansas. Kansas politician William Hutchinson said in an 1858 speech that "the building of railroads in Kansas has become to our country like the building of churches and school houses, one of the fixed emblems of civilization and national progress." Railroads connected Kansas river towns with inland communities, producers with consumers. As Hutchinson put it, they provided the "jugular vein to the commonwealth."[8]

Arthur Joel Bolinger's family was among the wave of midwesterners who settled in Kansas in the years after the Civil War ended. A. J. recalled that his father believed that prosperity would be found at the "end of a railroad." William Bolinger operated a series of general stores in the small railroad towns of southeastern Kansas. Born in Maryland in 1847, William migrated to Illinois with his family before eventually making his way to Kansas. William Bolinger married Delia Hostetter in Neosho County in 1871. According to the memoir, William first moved his bride to the village of Thayer, where they rented a four-room house and he ran a general store. At some point, he moved to Longton, where in 1881, his father-in-law, Joel Hostetter, joined him in the hardware and furniture business.[9]

A native of Ohio, Joel Hostetter had grown up in Indiana where he went into the dry goods business "as soon as he was old enough to reach the counter." Hearing of new opportunities in Kansas, in 1868 he migrated to Ottawa in the east central part of the state and opened a store. Four years later, he moved to Thayer, further south in Neosho County. In Thayer, Hostetter farmed and raised livestock. Sometime after this, Joel's daughter met and married William Bolinger, and the elder couple joined the younger family in Longton.[10]

Young A. J. was born February 2, 1881, joining his six-year-old brother Bill. He was born in Longton, one of the townships developed by a group of investors. Longton, located in Elk County in the state's southeastern corner, boasted a population of 10,623, according to the 1880 census.[11] The federal government had purchased the land that became Elk County from the Osage Indians in 1867 and offered it for sale for $1.25 an acre, somewhat less than the more fertile lands in the Neosho and Verdigris River Valleys of the four counties just to the east. The low prices apparently attracted speculators and town developers. In 1870, investors J. W. Kerr, J. C. Pinney, J. Hoffman, J. B. Roberts, James Reynolds, and "a Mr. Gardner" formed a company to organize the township of Elk Rapids twelve miles southeast of the county seat at Howard. Soon the town was renamed Longton. Two lines of the Atchison, Topeka & Santa Fe Railroad joined in the town, spurring development. By the time of A. J.'s birth, the township boasted a steam sawmill, a hardware store, a post office, a school, a newspaper, a two-story hotel, and a handful of other businesses to serve local farmers and railroad workers.[12]

Longton and its surrounding farms were in a relatively good location. Though the lands there may not have been as fertile as those in counties further east, rainfall averaged a healthy thirty-seven to forty-two inches per year in eastern Kansas, a sharp contrast to the paltry fifteen-inch averages found along the state's border with Colorado. Elk County was named for the Elk River, which dissects the county diagonally from northwest to southeast, and the county is well watered by streams. Fertile river and creek bottoms attracted settlers who hoped to farm. The area is sometimes nicknamed the "Kansas Ozarks," a moniker that can be misleading. Most of Elk County had gently rolling hills, not the steep small mountains of the

Ozarks. The Flint Hills dominate the extreme western edge of the county, where trees and rolling hills begin to disappear. While timber was not abundant in Elk County, enough hardwoods thrived along the county's rivers and streams to provide some building materials for the county's early settlers, a resource not available to settlers in the state's far western counties.[13]

William Bolinger and Joel Hostetter may have moved to Longton at the urging of town boosters who convinced them that Longton was on the verge of being a boomtown. Whatever they expected, Longton must have proved disappointing. When A. J. was five, William purchased a large ranch several miles outside Longton. Life proved difficult here, too. On the ranch, extreme weather plagued the family enterprise. Nature treated Kansas to furious extremes, a fact that made life precarious for farmers and merchants alike. Farming in Kansas was a fickle business. Wide variations in high and low temperatures took their toll on men and beasts. Devastating tornados—cyclones, in A. J.'s parlance—swept across the prairies, wiping out farmsteads and whole towns. In 1874, the year A. J.'s older brother, Bill, was born, a plague of "grasshoppers" (actually Rocky Mountain locusts) descended on most of the state, eating not only the crops in the field but also the clothing on drying lines and even the harnesses off horses. Millions of cattle froze to death during the severe blizzards of the 1880s, especially the "long" winter of 1880–1881 and the bitter winter of 1885–1886. Speculators promised that "rain follows the plow," insisting that settlement and farming would generate generous rainfall. Many settlers believed this; and indeed, rainfall was abundant through most of the 1870s and the early 1880s, and harvests were bountiful. In fact, floods frequently inundated farms along eastern Kansas's rivers and streams, as Bolinger vividly describes. By the 1880s, the principal cash crop in Kansas was Russian red winter wheat, a grain that could survive the region's harsh winters, but not unusual droughts. A severe drought that dragged on from 1884 to 1887 destroyed the notion that rain followed the plow and brought on a severe agricultural depression in the state.[14]

The 1880s drought coincided with a decline in farm prices. A. J. described those years as "hard days for the Kansas farmer." He recalled an occasion when his grandfather hauled a load of "ear corn" (unshelled corn) to town but returned home "to burn it in the kitchen stove in place of the purchased coal" because he was unable to sell the product at any price. Corn sold for more than sixty cents per bushel in 1881, but prices fell steadily throughout the decade, bottoming out in 1889 at ten cents per bushel.[15]

To make matters worse, most Kansas farmers were deeply in debt. Establishing a homestead on the prairies and plains was a capital-intensive proposition. Not only did most farmers purchase their land from speculators and railroads, often at inflated rates, but they also needed oxen and heavy plows to break the land. They required wagons and hand tools. They purchased building materials for construction of houses and barns that had to be shipped considerable distances. Lacking other sources of drinking water, they invested in wells. Because of all these expenses, most farmers borrowed money to get started. In addition, many of the state's more settled farmers, motivated by the prosperity of the 1870s and early 1880s, became speculators themselves. They borrowed money to buy additional land, banking that they could sell it for a large and easy profit. Farmers also faced high taxes. In order to finance railroad bonds and provide services, townships raised tax rates on town lots and farmsteads alike. The collapse in both farm prices and farm productivity levels of the mid-1880s was devastating to many in the Kansas countryside. One indicator of the distress was the growing number of farmers who lost their land and had to become tenants on land owned by others. In 1880, only 16 percent of Kansas farmers were tenants. By 1900, this figure had risen to 35 percent.[16]

To make matters worse, farmers now found themselves at the mercy of corporate entities that did not adjust their prices or practices to downturns in the agricultural marketplace. Farmers had once produced largely for local markets, shipping commodities no more than fifty or one hundred miles from their homes. But by the 1880s, most Kansas farmers were engaged in the production of crops and livestock for national commodities markets. Local markets simply could not absorb all the corn, wheat, and cattle produced in Kansas; farmers had no choice but to ship their products to distant markets via the railroad. Yet freight rates did not drop when grain prices dropped. Farmers complained about unfair railroad pricing practices.

Railroads were not the only corporations to raise farmers' ire. They also railed at banks for high interest rates and tight credit. Farmers complained about the high costs of farm equipment, accusing equipment manufacturers of profiteering. They claimed that grain elevators were parasites on the farmer because they bought low and sold high, making exorbitant profits without adding much value to the commodities.[17]

A combination of economic problems and changed market relations mobilized a massive and militant agrarian movement. During these years, Kansas voters began to call for government regulation to protect the interests of farmers, small businessmen, and consumers. Farmers organized chapters of the Patrons of Husbandry, commonly called the Grange, in the 1870s. The Grange protested high railroad rates and the heavy levels of municipal bonded debt that drove up local tax rates. The state legislature responded with a wave of regulations in the realms of business, public health, and social welfare, including the 1883 establishment of a Board of Railroad Commissioners charged with adjudicating disputes about railroad rates and practices. Conditions for farmers worsened, leading them to call for more drastic action.[18]

By the mid-1880s, Kansas farmers turned to a new and more radical organization founded in Texas. The Farmers' Alliance tried three approaches to improve the lives of its members. First, the organization functioned as an educational institution, bringing new knowledge about scientific agriculture to its local chapters, in hopes of helping farmers improve their productivity and profitability. Second, the Farmers' Alliance tried to free farmers from their dependence on the marketplace. Alliance members pooled their resources to purchase expensive farm equipment for communal use. They purchased seed and other supplies in bulk, enabling them to negotiate lower prices. Some Alliance chapters explored developing their own warehouses to hold nonperishable crops until market prices rose. Alliance members found that these methods had limited effectiveness, so the organization turned to a third strategy: political action.[19]

Alliance chapters campaigned for a host of reforms in Kansas to address outrageous railroad shipping fees, soaring interest rates, high taxes, and tax policies that placed a disproportionate burden on farmers. In their early forays into the political realm, Farmers' Alliance members supported candidates who were sympathetic to their demands, regardless of the candidate's party affiliation, but they gradually came to see the dominant political parties as hostile to their interests. In an attempt to broaden their political influence, in 1890 the Kansas Farmers' Alliance formed the People's Party, commonly called the Populists, two years before the birth of the national People's Party.[20]

At first the Populists enjoyed some success in Kansas. Populist leaders galvanized support among farmers by holding colorful rallies that included the whole family and used dramatic oratory. The most famous Populist speaker, and one of the most successful, was Mary Elizabeth Lease. She was born in Pennsylvania to Irish immigrant parents and came to Kansas to teach school when she was in her twenties. Lease gravitated to the Populist movement where she called for farmers to raise "less corn and more hell" and condemned "government of Wall Street, by Wall Street, and for Wall Street." Farmers loved Lease, and her anticorporate rhetoric resonated with their beliefs about the source of their troubles.[21]

Thanks to the efforts of organizers like Lease and to the growing frustration of farmers, Populists gained some ground in the Kansas legislature in the 1890s. In 1896, the state party joined the national party in allying themselves with the Democratic Party, which had included many Populist demands in its party platform. This was in part a response to the deepening economic crises of the 1890s; for Kansas farmers afflicted by low prices for their crops, high storage and railroad charges, and an unforgiving credit market, the "Gay 90s" were anything but gay, as Bolinger observed.[22]

While the United States had become an industrial power and the leading producer of iron and steel, the combination of depressed commodity prices, recurring and steadily more serious economic crises, and the erratic federal monetary and economic policies of the two Grover Cleveland administrations and the intervening Benjamin Harrison administration created a "Gilded Age" for some and hardship for many. By the time of the 1896 campaign that resulted in the election of William McKinley, following the economic crash of 1893, the United States had experienced a profound economic depression.[23]

The Democratic presidential candidate was famed attorney and orator William Jennings Bryan. Although Republican A. J. derided Bryan's "queer philosophy" of manipulating the monetary system with free coinage of silver, he admitted that the candidate was a spellbinding orator. He reported, "You hung on every word, and it seemed the very epitome of logic, but when you left the scene . . . to save your life you couldn't remember a thing you heard." To Bolinger's relief, Republican William McKinley defeated Bryan, and Populism faded away. Although it would never be a force in Kansas politics again, many Populist reform ideas lived on and were enacted during the Progressive era of the early twentieth century.

Although the sequence of events is unclear in the memoir, at some point in A. J.'s childhood, the family decamped from Longton for the town of Eureka, fifty miles north. The agrarian financial crisis of the late 1880s probably played some role in this decision. When farmers struggled, they were unable to patronize local merchants, a fact that would have taken a toll on William Bolinger's business. A. J. notes that the liquidation of the family's Longton store stock yielded barely enough to purchase a "rather poor prairie farm near Eureka," testimony to the sorry state of business affairs at the time. But he also offers two other reasons for the move. First was Prohibition. A vigorous Prohibition movement began in Kansas late in the 1870s and gained momentum throughout the period. Bolinger suggests that the wild nature of cow towns like Abilene helped spur the effort to restrict alcohol consumption. The legislature passed a Prohibition Amendment to the state constitution in 1879, which led to a heated campaign by both pro- and anti-prohibition forces attempting to sway voters prior to the general election. Kansas voters approved the amendment in November of 1880, and Kansas became a dry state on January 1, 1881. According to A. J., William Bolinger had campaigned for the Prohibition Amendment, earning him the ire of "a great majority of the people in this area." As a result, he lost customers, his business declining to the "point where, if they cleared up their business obligations, little or nothing would be left."[24]

The other reason he gives for the family's removal to Eureka was the dearth of educational opportunities in Longton for young Bill and A. J. Although Kansas had a proud tradition of commitment to public education, apparently the level of that commitment varied from place to place. A. J. described the Longton elementary schools as boasting "indifferent teaching quality." Delia Bolinger had been a teacher before her marriage, and she taught the boys through the early grades; but as they grew older, the family wanted to provide them with access to better schools. William Bolinger and some of his fellow citizens unsuccessfully attempted to establish a private academy in the town. At that point, the family looked north to Eureka, which possessed a good public school system, including a high school. It was also home to Southern Kansas Academy, operated by the Congregational Church, where A. J. and Bill enrolled. A. J. noted that the academy was intended to prepare students for the mission field, and it did produce a number of prominent missionaries, including Bishop John A. Gregg, a noted A.M.E. minister who served in the mission field in South Africa. The school also offered classical and scientific curricula intended to prepare young men for college.[25]

After the move, the Hostetter grandparents operated the new farm, while William Bolinger earned a living in Eureka as a sheet metal worker and the family set up housekeeping in a town rental. A. J. noted that his father was "never satisfied long to work for wages." With careful savings he accumulated enough capital in eighteen months' time to open his own general store and tinsmithing shop in Eureka.

A. J.'s descriptions of his years at Southern Kansas Academy and of small-town life in Eureka are some of the most vivid chapters in the book, likely because he was old enough during those years to have formed solid impressions and retained strong memories. Defying our image of dull life in a sleepy village, he details a vibrant social scene where women visited regularly and enjoyed organized gatherings like quilting bees, young people frolicked at Sunday School picnics and dance parties, and people of all ages attended political rallies and shows at the local "Oprey" houses.

Bolinger wrote, "It was as natural that I should enter Washburn College as for me to breathe. All S.K.A. men went to Washburn." Like Southern Kansas Academy, Washburn was affiliated with the Congregational Church. Washburn, which began as a hotbed of abolitionist sentiment in 1865, was originally named Lincoln College. In

1868, the college was renamed for Ichabod Washburn, a Massachusetts industrialist who made a $25,000 donation to the institution. A. J. matriculated in 1900, and the school provided a solid liberal arts curriculum that served him well as preparation for his later law studies. Washburn grew rapidly, adding a law school in 1903, just in time for aspiring attorney A. J. to enroll.[26]

To enable A. J.'s enrollment at Washburn, the family moved yet again, this time to Topeka. There, William Bolinger took over a business that sold musical instruments and sewing machines. A. J. noted that the prospects for success in the musical instrument business were rather poor but that his father persisted and ran the business until his retirement.

Stories of his college days in Topeka are as lively and detailed as those of his years at S.K.A. At Washburn College, A. J. became involved in the Prohibition movement that had proved fateful for his father fifteen years earlier. Though the state had passed a Prohibition Amendment in 1880, the enabling laws that accompanied the amendment were primarily directed at closing saloons rather than preventing the illicit manufacture and consumption of alcohol. Liquor dealers who paid regular fines to law enforcement officers ran illegal saloons known as "blind pigs." In 1883, two years after the amendment took effect, there were still forty open saloons in Topeka, and illegal operations prospered over the next two decades. As a result, temperance agitation revived around the turn of the century. Washburn's president from 1871 to 1895 was the Reverend Peter McVicar, and with its close affiliation with the Congregational Church, the school joined Topeka as a center of temperance agitation.[27]

One of the most famous of Kansas's temperance activists was Carry (or Carrie) Nation. Nation's first husband had been an alcoholic, sparking her disgust for alcohol consumption. While living in Kansas in 1900, she began her campaign. In addition to the traditional temperance activities of praying outside saloons and denouncing patrons of those establishments, she began vandalizing the liquor and furnishings of saloons. She became famous for "busting up" saloons with her trademark ax. A large woman (she was reputed to be six feet tall), she was a formidable adversary, but she was also arrested repeatedly and beaten more than once. A. J. and many of his friends joined a temperance group who aided Nation in breaking into Topeka saloons in a most dramatic fashion.

Inspired by the example of two Sunday School teachers whom he admired, young A. J. set out to become a lawyer. He began reading law in the office of one of the attorneys. Fortunately, Washburn opened a law school in 1903, and A. J. obtained approval to finish his last two years of his undergraduate program simultaneously with his first two years of law school. After two years of law study, Bolinger received a letter from a former classmate who had become well established as a banker in Oklahoma. The friend "begged me to come down and get admitted to the bar and practice in his town." With the confidence of youth, Bolinger felt well prepared to pass the bar exam, even without completing his final year of law school. More compelling, he was in love with Gertrude Ott, a fellow student he met during his junior year. He decided to take the bar exam, marry Gertrude, and establish his practice in Oklahoma. As he wrote, "At that time I was more interested in the degree P.F. (Pater Familias) than that Ll.B." Once he was admitted to the bar, he and Gertrude set up housekeeping in Weleetka, a village in east central Oklahoma. Founded in 1902, Weleetka was still very much a frontier town when the young couple arrived. Like Longton, Kansas, Weleetka was the site of the junction of two railroad lines, that of the Frisco Railroad and the Ft. Smith and Guthrie line. Here A. J. began a law practice, and soon, like his father, he became embroiled in local political intrigues.

As with Kansas, many Americans had viewed the territory that is now Oklahoma as unfit for white settlement. After the federal government assigned a number of eastern tribes to the area in the 1830s, Oklahoma was commonly, but mistakenly, dubbed "Indian Territory." In fact, the government assigned each tribe discrete territories, and they operated as independent tribal governments until almost the end of the century.[28]

In 1887, however, the passage of the Dawes Severalty (or General Allotment) Act signaled a radical shift in US Indian policy that would prove fateful for tribes in Oklahoma. The Dawes Act was intended to encourage Native American assimilation into the mainstream of American society, a move that had been advocated by so-called

Indian reformers for a number of years. In order to become "civilized," argued these reformers, Indians needed to adopt individual rather than communal property holding and settle into life as small farmers. Under the terms of the Dawes Act, reservation lands were broken into separate plots and distributed to individual Indian families. The land was to be held in trust by the federal government for twenty-five years, after which the successful farmers would receive a certificate of competency; but most of this land was not suitable for farming, making it impossible to succeed at earning a living as small farmers. Moreover, with no land to control, the authority of tribal governments was undermined. As two scholars put it, the Dawes Act was part of a federal policy "to eliminate tribal authority completely." Bolinger was blunter in his criticism of federal Indian policy when he wrote, "Looking back at the history of the white man's transactions with the Indians is not something which could rightly be said to create pride in our national honor."[29]

The reservation land not allotted to individual Native American families was opened to homesteaders for settlement. In 1889 Congress authorized the opening of two million acres of "surplus" lands in the so-called Indian Territory to homesteading. On April 22, 1889, fifty thousand people gathered on the border between Kansas and the Indian Territory awaiting the pistol shot that would leave them free to race into the region and claim the choicest lands. This was the first of the legendary Oklahoma "land rushes." Bolinger and his family may have witnessed this event or a later land run. Soon the white population of the state soared. In 1890, Congress established the Oklahoma Territory in unorganized areas of what is now central Oklahoma.[30]

By 1905 when Bolinger set up his law practice in Oklahoma, Congress had passed enabling legislation that joined the so-called Indian Territory, a southeastern zone known as the Cherokee Strip, and the Oklahoma Territory to form the state of Oklahoma. State leaders were authorized to write and ratify a constitution and organize counties and congressional districts in order to complete the process of admission to the Union, which was accomplished in 1907.[31]

Bolinger "plunged right into the middle of things" in Weleetka's battle to become the county seat of Okfuskee County. The other contenders were the towns of Henrietta and Okemah. A. J. describes the political battle in some detail, noting that "any means, trickery, violence, outright bribery were legitimate tools" in the county seat fight. To help Weleetka gain ground, local leaders asked Bolinger to begin publishing a Democratic newspaper, having heard that he had worked on the college paper at Washburn. Okfuskee County was predominantly Democratic, but the local paper was Republican. "A dyed in the wool, born, bred, and reared Republican," A. J. nonetheless seized the opportunity because it offered a chance for "gaining acquaintance over the area."[32]

Bolinger received frequent threats of violence during the county seat fight. At the same time, he was busy building a practice, gaining litigation experience, and becoming a father. (Son Dwight was born in 1907.) But the county seat fight would shape his career. Weleetka lost the battle to Okemah. Knowing that he would need to move his practice to the county seat if he remained in Okfuskee County, something he did not want to do, and knowing as well that "I had made enemies of about all the people in the other two communities," A. J. decided it would be prudent to return to Topeka and practice law there.

A. J. practiced law in Topeka from the time of his return from Oklahoma after 1907 until early 1916. In the 1967 manuscript and in an audio reminiscence he recorded between 1967 and 1969, A. J. expresses satisfaction at the success of his law practice in Topeka, observing in the manuscript that he was "blessed with reasonable success; not near the successes of my dreams, yet not nearly as bad as it might have been."[33] A brief review of some of his cases that reached appellate courts shows that his practice was varied, including railroad employer liability cases, domestic disputes, and civil service matters.[34]

As he had during his boyhood, A. J. continued to travel for business and for pleasure. These trips occasionally led to encounters, albeit brief, with legendary figures from American history. For example, on a trip to Washington, DC, in 1909 to visit his brother William, who at the time was working for the Census Bureau, A. J. was persuaded to join the crowd at Ft. Myer in Virginia on one late July day. He had been told that there would be a demonstration of a new and dangerous device, the aeroplane. He and his brother traveled to Ft. Myer—as did President Taft and many others—to witness one of the early commercial demonstration flights of Orville Wright. A. J. witnessed on July 27, 1909, the most successful of what were termed the "Army Trials," where Wright and passenger Lt. Frank Lahm flew for just over one hour, reaching speeds in excess of forty miles per hour, and negotiating the course from Ft. Myer to Alexandria and back. At the time, A. J. considered such flight foolishly dangerous. In fact, a trial at the same spot just months earlier had resulted in the first air fatality—Wright's passenger—and serious injuries to Wright. Nonetheless, the incident demonstrates A. J.'s uncanny knack for being in the right place at the right time to witness historic events.[35]

The 1915 Kansas census shows A. J., his wife Gertrude, and their son Dwight living in Topeka. On November 1, 1915, A. J.'s beloved Gertrude died.[36] A. J. continued his practice and cared for his son. In early 1916, A. J. moved from Topeka to Kansas City, where he would stay for approximately four years.

On August 16, 1916, A. J. married Ella B. Harrison in New London, Missouri. While he established his legal practice in Kansas City, he remarked in his audio reminiscence that he left Kansas City after four years because "I didn't like the city very well."[37]

In 1919 the Bolingers moved to Morgan County, in central Missouri, where Bolinger was able to escape the city and try his hand at farming. In this, he repeated the pattern of his childhood that one reads about in this memoir, that of moving from rural to urban and back to rural settings. His daughter Margaret Ruth Bolinger was born while they resided on the farm.

A. J.'s daughter Mary recalls her father telling her years later that he abandoned farming within a year or so because of losses suffered from catastrophic floods—again, a repetition of early childhood experiences recounted in the memoir.[38] As a result, A. J. moved his family from farm to town, though one more like the Kansas towns of his youth than the cities of his early adulthood. He moved to Versailles, the seat of Morgan County, where he established a law practice, becoming a key member of the community and remaining in the same home until his death in 1977. His son William Harrison Bolinger was born not long after, in 1921, and four years later his final child, Mary

Ella Harrison Bolinger, second wife of A. J. Bolinger,
picture taken in Kansas City, circa 1916–1918.
(Photograph courtesy of Mary Bolinger Barker)

Julia Bolinger, arrived. By then, his first son, Dwight, was away at school and home only during the summer.

The years after 1925 were filled with family, work, and politics, but they were also filled with music, outdoor adventures, and poetry. When the Lake of the Ozarks was constructed as a flood control and recreation project just south of Versailles, A. J. was one of the first to build a retreat at the lakeshore. The Lake of the Ozarks opened in 1931, and not long after, A. J. built what he termed a "log cottage," taking his family to the lake for adventures in an early motorboat (powered, he recalled, by an old automobile engine).[39] His delight

James Harrison (Ella's father); Dwight Bolinger, A. J.'s son by his first wife; and A. J. Bolinger, circa 1920s. (Photograph courtesy of Bruce Bolinger)

in outdoor activities was complemented by an intellectual life made possible by the excellent education he received at the Southern Kansas Academy and at Washburn College. In 1966 A. J. published a book of original poetry, *Mine Eyes Unto the Hills: An Ozark Anthology*, which has been cited as an important work in the Ozark folk tradition.[40]

A. J.'s law practice continued through the 1930s. He became a judge in Morgan County in 1941, a position he held until the late 1960s. His son William went into the law after World War II, serving as prosecuting attorney and probate court judge in Morgan County. Eventually, father and son rejoined each other in a private law practice that continued until very near the end of A. J.'s life in 1977.

As delightful as A. J. Bolinger's memoir is, he leaves the reader wanting more. He is largely silent about his relationships with family members. He says a great deal about his father's business and farming enterprises, but we are left to draw conclusions about William Bolinger the man from tantalizing hints in comments about the elder man's perseverance and ambition and his commitment to his son's

A. J. and three of his children, circa 1920s. *From left to right:* Dwight Bolinger, Mary Julia Bolinger, Margaret Ruth Bolinger, A. J. (Photograph courtesy of Mary Bolinger Barker)

education. We learn almost nothing about the maternal grandparents who were so much a part of his childhood.

Writing in the 1960s, A. J. offers barbed comments about young women in general, but he is largely silent about his relationships with the women in his life. We learn little more about Delia Hostetter Bolinger than that she was a teacher before her marriage and that she taught her sons in their early years. Although he never says so

Arthur Joel Bolinger with his three children by his second wife, Ella Harrison Bolinger, no date (circa early 1930s). *Children from left to right:* Mary Julia Bolinger, William H. Bolinger, and Margaret Ruth Bolinger. (Photograph courtesy of Bruce Bolinger)

explicitly, he clearly adored Gertrude Ott. He describes her as being smarter than himself and a talented musician, and he relished the welcoming home she created. Perhaps this silence is due to the sorrow of her early death.

To a historian of women's history, this silence about the women in his life is particularly frustrating because the history of women

A. J. and Ella Bolinger's three children, circa 1930s. *From left to right:* Mary Julia, Margaret Ruth, and William H. The picture hanging on the wall in the background is a childhood portrait of A. J. Bolinger, later lost in a fire. (Photograph courtesy of Mary Bolinger Barker)

in Kansas is a lively and fascinating one. Historians of the American West have noted that women's work was crucial to survival in frontier regions and have hypothesized that women's centrality to the frontier enterprise helped them leverage more political power. Whatever the cause, Kansas had a strong women's rights movement. The state had liberal laws regarding married women's control of their property and rights to guardianship of children. Women gained the right to vote in school board elections in the territory in 1859, and they became the first state to consider (but reject) full female suffrage in 1867. Kansas women gained full municipal suffrage and the right to hold municipal office in 1887.[41]

Kansas women were also active in all kinds of reform movements. As western communities became more settled, women played important roles in organizing schools, churches, and voluntary associations. As historian Julie Roy Jeffrey has put it, "In the West, 'the cult of domesticity,' with its insistence on female service could be stretched to expand women's moral and cultural responsibilities. . . . Women

A. J. Bolinger on horseback, circa 1950s.
(Photograph courtesy of Mary Bolinger Barker)

served families and communities by maintaining social values, molding behavior, and preserving culture." How much more we would like to know about all of Bolinger's personal relationships.[42]

Probably his reticence in speaking of those he loved most was in keeping with his character. His daughter Mary Bolinger Barker described him as a quiet and generous man. He was an affectionate man who brought his children special treats from Kansas City when he traveled there for business, took them on hikes and to his law office, and emphasized the value of education in their lives, but he did not often tell stories about his childhood. In fact, she noted that she learned a lot of things about her father that she had not known by reading the memoir years after his death. Since A. J. wrote the memoir in response to urging from his eldest son, Dwight, it is likely that he had not spent his life dwelling on his childhood memories.[43]

A. J. began life in a simple prairie home, with horses and dogs and hard work. He experienced the tumult of America in the 1880s and 1890s, saw Orville Wright fly a primitive airplane, lived through two World Wars (and numerous others), and lived to fly on modern jets to visit his daughter in southern California. His childhood was

A. J. Bolinger in his office, circa 1960s. (Photograph courtesy of Mary Bolinger Barker)

without automobiles, electric power, or modern communications; he lived to see the development of computers and watch humans land on the moon. Through this incredible period of change, a character emerges, one that gives us insight into a particularly American experience.

When Mari Sandoz published the portrait of her father, Nebraska pioneer Jules Sandoz, the picture that emerged was of a tough, even bitter man who faced a harsh environment with a hard, ruthless sense of reality and little tolerance for anything or anyone else.[44] A. J. Bolinger's origins in the same era and environment produced a very different man and a very different picture of the prairie experience at the closing of the frontier. A. J. was no stranger to violence and suffering, as the memoir shows, but he drew from his experience a thoughtful, gentle, and even poetic nature, a love of the "bluestem prairie," and a lasting sense of the joys of life.

A Note on Editorial Method

Arthur J. Bolinger's writing was clear, sharp, precise, and logical. Although he occasionally drifts a bit in his reminiscences, he always comes back to his main point. We have seen little need to edit his work extensively. In transcribing the original manuscript, which he produced on a manual typewriter, we have endeavored to make as few changes as possible. We have occasionally added commas for clarity, placed missing words in brackets, or corrected a misspelling that might lead to misreading, but otherwise, the text appears as he wrote it. We have added endnotes to annotate many of his historical references. Our goal has been to provide the reader with only the most basic information, but you may consult the sources that we list for additional details.

As we note in the introduction, at times A. J. Bolinger displayed progressive thinking that was unusual for people of his generation. His use of the English language was nonetheless a product of his own times, and his choice of terms to denote racial and ethnic identity was consistent with common terminology in his era. His use of the words "Negro" and "colored" to refer to African Americans and "Indian" to refer to Native Americans reflected the polite usage of his own day.

We have retained his word choices for historical accuracy in keeping with our treatment of the rest of his manuscript.

Additional fragments of the memoir were found among the supporting manuscript. They were written later, apparently at Dwight Bolinger's behest, and they did not fit into A. J.'s original organizing scheme for the memoir. Because they seemed to interrupt the flow of his narrative, we have not included them here, though we did draw on some of that material in the introduction.

CHAPTER 1

Background in General

At last the spirit moves me.

For a long time my children and grandchildren have been urging me to commit to paper the tales of the olden days with which I amused their childhood. Now I yield to their urging, or more perhaps to indulge an old man's vanity; in recounting the days of my youth.

I was born on February 2nd, 1881 in the little town of Longton, in Elk County Kansas.[1] Not that this date is one of world shaking importance; but we have to commence somewhere and perhaps that is as good as any.

To understand a people, I have always said; you must know something about their environment. In this, as far as the Midwest is concerned, America, east of Indiana, is as profoundly ignorant as they are of the tribal customs and ethics of an inhabitant of Mars.

In the first place one speaks of the Great Plains, and the easterner at once visualizes a vast area of flat, barren and uninteresting desert as far as the eye can reach. That is not really true of any part of the plains, but least of all the Eastern part of Kansas. There the scene is not much different from that of the Missouri Ozarks, though the hills have been smoothed out a bit, and timber is found only along the streams. The hills themselves were in that day, and to some extent still are clothed in blue stem grass; a tall strong grass; so tall that a rider going through it on horseback, was hidden until only his body from the waist up, and his horse's head, was visible. This grass was so rich in sugar that it was possible to produce cattle ready for market just by a summer's grazing. One of the finest sights, was and still is, the cattle upon a thousand hills. Now only white face or Angus, then the many hued longhorn, red, white, roan, spotted, lank, rangy, and fleet of foot.

My home was only about 15 miles off the first Chisholm Trail but since the coming of partly sufficient rail transportations the herds were no longer driven overland, but were shipped in train load after train load, from Texas to Kansas for the summer's graze.[2]

These wild herds were always interesting. And their unloading and handling was always full of excitement. From the trains they were unloaded into pens; and to restrain them required a sturdy construction. The fences about these pens were made of two inch lumber, braced and cross braced and from eight to ten feet high, usually with a footboard so that an observer could stand and see clearly the work in the pens. It was nothing to see a wild Texas steer attempt to jump out; and in a few occasions, impossible as it might seem, I have seen them succeed. And small wonder.

From the pen into which they were unloaded from the car, they had to pass one at a time through a narrow chute one side of which was moveable, so that it could be pressed against the animal; then men swarmed about him. The long vicious horns were sawed off, one man to each horn, another man applied the ranch man's brand, and bulls were castrated. The whole operation took about two minutes.

Some of the other affairs at the pens were less bloody. Our saddle stock came mostly from the wild herds in Wyoming and Montana. When a load of ponies arrived we really did have sport. You could buy a pony for five dollars, and then give a wrangler five dollars more to ride him. Vastly different from our present day rodeos, which are its illegitimate offspring, the purpose was not to madden and ruin a horse; but to train him and make him a useful companion. He was ridden to a standstill and was then turned over to his new owner. Of course for quite a while he had to be rebroken every morning, but eventually he settled down into his work and liked it. The old time cow pony really loved working cattle. My own favorite mount in my teens was a little "flea bitten" pony, about 14 hands high[3] and with the letter "T" almost as big as she was branded on her right shoulder. Used as a cutting horse, that is to separate some particular animal and bring it out of the herd, and she was in her glory. Put her at some particular beast, guiding her until she had seen the one you wanted, then you need only guide her by swaying your body. Teeth snapping, she was after that poor steer, and squirm and twist as he might, there was no avoiding her guidance. My complaint of the modern rodeo, is that it is inhumanely cruel and useless. In place of training as his friend, the horse is tortured until frantic with pain and then goaded by some prize grabbing acrobat is steered about the ring, Spanish spurs gouging and cutting him at every jump, and a flank strap of narrow cutting leather drawn tight around his flanks until he is in agony. The object not, as I said, to train, but to torture and make a noble and naturally gentle animal into a furious demon.

Usually my home was in towns; but even when not living on a ranch, as we sometimes did, my playmates and school mates were largely ranch children. We learned to ride early and well, and often accompanied drives not as paid drovers, but just for the sport of it and were usually assigned to the duty post of drag.[4] Even when robbed of their horns, a means of lessening fight damage in the herds, these long horns were mean and ornery, and woe be to the foolish man who got into a bunch of them on foot without ready means of escape. I well recollect one summer day when my older brother went hunting and did not return as expected, to the great alarm of my parents. He came dragging in about nine o'clock reporting that he had been chased by the cattle, and had to take refuge in a tree, and stay there long after sun down, waiting for them to go to their usual bedding ground, so it would be safe for him to come down from his perch.

I have mentioned how high the blue stem grew. It was burned off early each spring to give the new grass a chance to emerge and one of the most spectacular sights was to watch long lines of flames, sometimes ten miles in length, marching across the hills. At that time roads were not laid out. You went on a beeline wherever you wished. And every traveler, whether he smoked or not, carried with him a little bundle of matches. These to be able to start a fire in case one was suddenly caught in the path of an approaching prairie fire; which might well be fatal to both horse and rider as the flames sweeping through the tangle of long grass would reach as high as twenty feet from the ground. The safety measure was to take a match and start a fire downwind and so burn off a patch into which you could ride in safety before the main fire reached you. And these matches! Our modern kitchen match had not yet been introduced. What we carried was a sulfur match, about the same length as our present match, but tipped on the end with a little patch of phosphorous, followed up the stem for about a quarter of its length with sulfur. You lit the match by striking the phosphorous tip until it blazed and ignited the sulfur, then you waited until the fire had quit burning blue and turned red and it was ready for use. In all this time the sulfur had been sending up stinking fumes, like the atmosphere of tophet.[5]

These were days of great change. The last two decades of the nineteenth century, and the first decade of the twentieth, was a transition period. The old wild west, which was never as wild as the dime novels, the horse operas and the TV writers would have us believe; had calmed down. In my boyhood I personally knew many of the old time pioneer characters, but in my day, they had become respected and quiet citizens. And to me, they appeared no different than a grown man would be to a boy today. In fact most of the tales told of those frontier days are ridiculous to one who was a part of them. I have often said that if a woman had gone on the streets dressed as pictured on the TV she would have been arrested and run out of town. Of all the women in the westerns, I have found only one woman who always dressed as a woman of that era dressed. That is Miss Kitty in "Gunsmoke."[6] She has always been above reproach. Stretch pants such as some of the screen pretties wear, mannish attire in general would have stamped the wearer, if she was to wear them at all, as a person of ill repute. In fact it was at this time that a lady doctor in New York assumed men's attire to make it easier in her work, and was given a jail term as a recompense.[7] In fact at one time the state of Kansas handled this flair officially. There was solemn and duly enacted a statute, passed by house and senate and duly signed by the governor, which required all skirts to extend at least three inches below the patella (knee cap).[8]

Kansas was in 1880 embarking upon its dream of prohibition.[9] The saloon had disappeared, and the thirsty soul could find his only relief in a trip down an alley, and into the back door of the livery stable or some other secret place. This strictness was gradually eroded until by 1902 at the coming of Carrie Nation the state was almost wide open.[10] P.C., that is Post Carrie the state took on another of its sanctimonious eras. It was a criminal offense even to possess liquor of any sort, even purchased in adjoining and wet Missouri. This sanctimonious attitude was specially a product of certain political figures who made fine campaign material out of their dryness. In fact it was the common saying that one certain Sheriff in Shawnee County Kansas was so dry he had to prime his throat if he wanted to spit.

My father was never a man to believe in a pot of gold at the end of a rainbow. It was his sincere belief that it was at the end of a railroad. As a result his business traveled westward with the traveling of railroad construction and my family got to see most of the towns in southeastern Kansas. One of our stops was at Thayer; of which more at a later time.

I have told you that the true old west was not at all like the modern image. But the men and women of that age were far more heroic, though not as glamorous as the synthetic variety. The cowboy was simply a farm hand on horseback; and not too much different from any other farm laborer. He had to put up with hardships, but then so did everyone. Food was scarce, except for some kinds of game, and hard to come by. Most people raised, cured and preserved their fruits, meats and vegetables. Running water, electricity, telephones and the like were not only unknown, but undreamed of. Ice was a luxury you sometimes found in the larger towns. But with it all, home life was good. The family gathered about a table of an evening. That table was usually stocked with popcorn, apples, or taffy. One of the group could read aloud to the rest, or there was always Euchre or Pitch or perhaps dominoes or checkers. A boy could meet a lady on the street and recognize her as his mother, and remember her good night the night before. Would we could say the same today.

A. J. Bolinger as an infant, 1881.
(Photograph courtesy of Bruce Bolinger)

Speaking of a boy and his mother, I always remember how I hated to go shopping with my mother, but I always had to go and carry the bundles. Mother needed both hands, one to hold her parasol and the other to hold her long skirts out of the dust. Those skirts were not unusually long, but the general fashion of the time. I remember how a waggish barber whose shop was in a corner building, taught his parrot a nasty trick that caused a lot of local amusement and much embarrassment to visiting ladies. It was considered a shame if a woman in crossing a street pulled up her skirt hem to expose any of her nether limbs above the anklebone. The visiting ladies were enraged, as they crossed the street to hear a raucous voice, screaming "Show your leg! Show your leg," only to discover when they looked around that the words came from a parrot whose cage hung in the barber shop door.

Well, I have gotten myself safely born, which after all in those days of few doctors and no hospitals was a not inconsiderable feat;[11] I have given you a few hints of the times; bursting with energy, wild with ambition; utterly convinced of the manifest destiny of our nation; and not suffering from any of the gloomy premonitions that destiny has imposed upon us at this day.

Now I think I'll proceed to special instances, which are of course the things I told my children.

CHAPTER 2

The Town of Thayer

The little village of Thayer, in the eighteen seventies, was just a group of three or four hundred people, standing rather barren, just about seventy-five miles northwest of the southeast corner of the State of Kansas.[1] Typically, it consisted of a number of small frame houses, three or four rooms, and on some the paint already almost sanded off by the dusts of the Kansas winds. The business district, if it could be called such, was a group of four or five false front, one-story frame buildings. Boardwalks ran along the storefronts and in some places were also in front of the better homes. Other places the walkway was a path, fairly good in good weather, otherwise deep in dust or slippery in wet.

It was to this village that my father brought my mother after their marriage. Here he had a general store, and they rented a four-room house. They were a bit better than average in their home, for since screens had not yet been invented, or at least not marketed in the west, in summer time every home was fly infested. I can remember for months later diners were protected by a small boy standing at the table and waving a branch of some kind, peach if possible, for it

William Bolinger, father of Arthur Joel Bolinger, circa 1880s–1890s. William Bolinger was born in Maryland in 1847. (Photograph courtesy of Bruce Bolinger)

was light and thickly leafed. I even performed that service myself at windows so they could be raised and admit the air.

The events I am about to record happened before my time; but so much have I heard them discussed, that they have become as it were a part of my own memory.

Summer of 1874 began with a promise of good crops and propitious weather. The field crops were well along, corn laid bye, trees heavy with half grown fruit. There was no hint of disaster.

Brother Bill was 6 months old, and as usual he was playing on a folded blanket right in front of the open door, where he could have the benefit of whatever breezes were stirring.

Suddenly Mother was surprised at his shouting and laughing; so much that she stepped to the door herself. On looking, at first she could see nothing, then high in the sky she caught sight of what at first looked like a black cloud approaching. Bits of the cloud broke off and hurtled earthward; far differently than any cloud she had ever seen before. And then it began. The bombardment of the house at first like hail stones, then with a continuous hum; and the netting on the doors and windows were covered with insects. The grasshoppers had arrived.

This was the first year that Kansas had had to endure this pest. There was damage now and then of crops by heavy infestations of hoppers, but this was an invasion of an army. Everything was edible. They chewed to shreds handles of tools left outside, where they had been wet with perspiration. They devoured the peaches on the trees, together with the foliage, leaving the naked peach stones dangling on the naked boughs. Crops vanished from the fields, as though mowed. The only thing that seemed to prosper was poultry. Never were there such fat hens and turkeys, nor so many eggs. Otherwise the year's labor was a total loss. There was no feed for livestock. There was no wheat or corn for a meal. Messages of distress flew east, and Kansas Relief stations were set up in many places. A few farmers, like my grandfather, who was farming near Thayer, had foresight, as soon as the blue stem which, after the hoppers had run their cycle, put forth new growth. As soon as this grass was high enough to mow, they went forth on the open prairie and mowed and cured the hay, and filled their mows, and stacked in stack after stack outside and that winter their stock wintered well. But they were too few by far, and in most instances horses and cattle died of hunger.

Kansans were taught what it meant to ask charity, or rather to be forced to accept it, for many and astonishing were the things that were in the relief barrels of clothing. Some of it must have been reposing in attics since the Mexican war.[2] One group in the east purchased and sent to Thayer a barrel of salt meat. It was most gladly received and served with relish on man's tables, only to discover at the bottom of the barrel, a horse hoof with the shoe still firmly nailed thereto.

No Kansan whose family endured this plague will ever forget the tales that were told about it, nor the suffering it caused.[3]

The other matter which in a way made Thayer famous or perhaps infamous was the fact that it was the nearest town of any consequence to the Tavern operated by the Bender family. With that tavern was connected as lurid a piece of sensational news as was ever dreamed by Nick Carter[4] or any of the other writers of the dime novel era.

At this time, emigration toward the west was still quite largely by wagon. Travel by rail was expensive and many places unobtainable. The covered wagons in use at that time were not the huge Conestoga wagons of the traders' trains. They were simple farm wagons, two side boards high, and with a canvas cover. There were four bent wooden bows slipped into sets of slots on the outside of the wagon box, and over these were stretched the strong, white canvas, securely tied down at the sides and with a drawstring that could close either or both ends. The driver's seat could be placed inside this cover, or by moving it forward to the front end of the wagon, and the driver using a foot board attached to the front, he could be outside the wagon and the inside front closed. This was the preferred way; for most of these emigrants had to bring with them household goods, as much as they possessed; some farm tools, perhaps a plough tied on one side; a crate of chickens fastened at the back end, and a cow trailing at the end of a rope. Naturally progress was slow and night stops frequent. To accommodate such travelers, some farmers put up additional room and accepted guests for the night.

The Bender place was such a tavern. A large, rough, frame house of one huge room, on the first floor, divided by a curtain stretched across it midway, one end serving as a living and dining room and the other as a kitchen. The upstairs held one large room used as a combination bedroom for the family, and the other as a room for travelers. There was a shed room at one side which could also be called into service if needed, but was usually used as a storage place.

The family was German, the mother and father speaking with a pronounced accent. There was a grown son and daughter. They had obtained a great reputation for piety, for it was almost a constant sight to see papa Bender, sitting in a kitchen chair tilted back against the wall close to the front door, and with a German Bible open before his apparently deeply interested eyes.

The tavern was on a much traveled road leading between two important towns, Parsons, and Neodesha, about midway, and was well located to catch travelers on their first night out from Parsons on their westward trek.[5] There was nothing thought of this place, other than many of its like, until more and more people traveling west failed to arrive at their destination. They could be traced as far as Parsons, and then the trail went blank.

So persistent grew these rumors that attention was directed ever more sharply at the Benders. One man coming from the East was so persistent that the Benders took flight. They were there one day and the next gone. Immediate investigation showed the yard at the Bender tavern to be a well-occupied burial ground. Some of the victims were identified; some were not; and many more who had disappeared were never found.

Nor were the Benders ever heard of again; and their complete disappearance was one of the most highly discussed mysteries of the time, not only locally but throughout the United States. How they could so completely disappear was beyond comprehension, with all the publicity given them and their crimes.

The wounds on the victims led to the supposition that their death had occurred in this manner: The dining table was placed quite close to the curtain dividing the room and the guest would be seated with his back to the curtain so that when he would lean back a trifle it would push back onto the curtain. While mama and papa and sister Kat entertained the guest brother would slip into the kitchen and when the guest leaned back and his head bulged the curtain brother would crush it with a conveniently placed sledge hammer.

As I said, no one ever knew what became of the Benders. But there has arisen of late years a legend, reasonable in its sound, that the citizens of Neodesha formed a posse and started to the Bender place, and met them as they attempted to escape. That complete and summary justice was done on the spot; the Bender property destroyed and scattered and that their evil remains now repose in some spot near the scene of their crimes; truly unloved, but not forgotten.[6]

This may be a grizzly way to commence these tales. But they will give you a glimpse of the real bad men of that day; not heroic rascals marching bravely to face a show down and possible death; but sordid beasts, much as now, slinking through the night and striking from the rear.

CHAPTER 3

Early Recollections

Much has been said as to the amount of recollection of a child. Some claim that nothing is really remembered before the fifth year; that what seems to be remembered are occurrences that have been frequently discussed in the family, and a memory built up in that way. To this I cannot agree. My very earliest recollection is of a hot summer day, and my lying upon a quilt spread under a tall pine tree. How I lay there and wondered if that tree held up the clouds, as it seemed to do. Now I know that we left the farm where this occurred when I was between three and four years old. My parents built a house in town and I can remember riding there in my baby carriage and still see the fringe on the canopy top fluttering in the breeze. And between the memory of the pine tree and our removal to the new house lies another memory.

At this time I was the owner of a black and tan rat terrier named Frankie; and I was inordinately proud of him and his exploits. His ratting ability was well known. I remember that at one time the oldest livery barn was being torn down to give room for a newer one. These barns all had heavy wooden floors, and under the floors were always colonies of rats. The crew doing the wrecking asked my brother and

I to bring Frankie to see what he could do, to care for the game when the floor was torn up.

When the first plank was pulled up the rats began to scurry out in every direction, and Frankie went into action. He didn't tarry over one victim when there was danger of another escaping, but he'd seize one by the back of the neck, give it a quick bite and shake it and throw it down and proceed to the next. He kept that up until the entire floor had been pulled up; and they gathered up of his victims a full wheelbarrow load.

However, my last experience with Frankie was a much sadder affair.

Our farm was divided by the Elk river, a stream of considerable size; and the farm house stood not far from the river bank, with the barn still nearer, so as to be easily accessible for stock water. This made it convenient for that purpose but there were drawbacks[1] to this too.

But the place was a wonderful playground for two small boys and their dog. Brother Bill was 10 and I was three that summer. We would go some times to the barn and tilt the feed barrels and let Frankie take care of any rats or mice that might be hidden there. This particular day Bill tilted the barrel and I stooped down to peer under and drive out anything thereunder. This time it was not a rat, but a huge copperhead snake, coiled and ready to strike. It could not have missed my face but for one thing; Frankie saw, and in place of beating a hasty retreat as he might have done, jumped for the snake's head just as it lunged at me. He was bitten savagely in the face. Brother Bill dropped the barrel on the snake which had come part way out from under, and pinioned it until he could get a hoe and kill it. But poor Frankie was already feeling the effects of the deadly venom. We tried every remedy but there was no help. For a long time the grave of little Frankie was a place to which I went quite regularly with floral tributes.

Small towns of that day had few amusements. After we moved from the farm, we were often put to it to find a pass time. But one thing was always welcome. Longton was the terminal town on the Howard Branch Railroad. Trains, or so we called them, though usually made up of just one passenger car and a combination smoking car and express car, and a small engine, of the type now shown in the television program called "Iron Horse."[2] But that was a link with the big, unknown outside world. They would come to the station, uncouple the cars and run the little engine on a turn table, and turn it around by man power for the trip back. Sunday afternoons we would be on hand. We came to know the crew and some times the engineer would let us ride in the engine cab during the turning process, and even let us put a hand on the magic throttle and help him.

My only run away experience was to sneak off one afternoon and go to the depot; where my mother, guessing my destination when she missed me, found me snuggly ensconced on the fireman's seat in the cab. I said that was my first run away. I was most thoroughly convinced on my return home, that such an experience was not worth the cost. That was the time when parents honestly believed that to spare the rod was to spoil the child. And I can't recollect where we ever loved them less because of their correction.

Sometimes my parents used good commonsense psychology by letting us do the things we threatened and suffer the consequences. I can well remember one such instance.

My father was at that time in the hardwood and implement business and had many country trips to see after the proper handling of the machinery, and the like. It was my delight to get a chance to ride along. For these trips he used a single horse between the shafts of a road cart. This was a two wheeled vehicle entered from the back by a step on the axle. It was very light and easy to handle and was capable of getting around in places that a four wheeled rig could have a hard time in making.

One hot summer day I was on one of these trips and on the return knowing that we had to cross a slough where there was always a place that horses wanted to drink, I mentioned to my father that as hot as it was old Charlie would certainly want to stop. This place was only a short way out of town and I now realize that father was in a hurry and didn't want to stop. At that he said "Art, I'll bet you a dollar against what's in your piggy bank that he won't drink." Ah ha! thinks I. Here's a chance to make a dollar easily; so I accepted the bet. What father did was when we came to the slough ford, was to leave Charlie's head held up by the checkrein, and drive directly on through. To say that I was outraged is a comparatively mild expression. I shouted "You didn't play fair! I hate you and I'm not riding another step with you!" I whirled around and crawled over the low rail on the road cart seat and dropped to the ground and sat down. Father never hesitated, but kept on jogging along; and one thing etched on my memory never to fade is the sight of father calmly jogging away and getting smaller and smaller. I couldn't stand it any longer, and bursting into tears I ran top speed toward the retreating cart. Father must have been expecting me, for I hadn't taken many steps until he turned around and drove back for me. I climbed aboard and neither of us said anything; but I learned quite sharply that it is always advisable to consider your conduct beforehand.

I realize full well, that to many, these simple tales of which I write, will seem trivial and unimportant. Trivial they are of course, but unimportant, no. All our lives are a woven pattern of trivial things. To so few is it given to accomplish any act of world importance. But woof and web of life, its seemingly trivial affairs, make up and shape the evolution of society. A wrong stitch here and a wrong tension there, can well warp and twist the pattern of the whole. Let us always hope that the pattern of what you esteem our trivial affairs may blend into and achieve the purpose of the great weaver.

One of these trivial things I will always remember was my first horse back ride. Of course at that time everyone rode and drove horses. So it was as natural for a child to yearn to ride as it is at present for him to wish to guide a car or steer an airplane.

My grandfather was a breeder and seller of horses. His ideal horse was one that was shapely, not too large and clumsy, fit for riding or driving either one, and of a tractable disposition. With that wish his choice fell upon the sturdy, reliable Morgan. This horse originated from a sire that had been used in logging operations in New England. He stood 14 ½ to 15 hands,[3] was most frequently bright bay, with flowing black mane and tail, and with a beautiful clean cut head, with small alert ears. By some mischance one of his colts was foaled a pure white albino. She was a filly,[4] unusually attractive and grandfather decided to keep her for his own use. She became a family pet and served principally as a buggy and saddle horse, doing light work. And she gained a deeper place in our hearts one winter

Johann Gottlieb (John G.) Bolinger, paternal grandfather of Arthur Joel Bolinger, no date. Born in Germany, Johann Gottlieb Bolinger was a tinsmith and is pictured here with some of the tools of his trade. (Photograph courtesy of Bruce Bolinger)

afternoon when she brought my mother's little sister home through a sudden blizzard where there were no roads to guide, and only her instinct coupled with the help of the Dalmatian dog which usually accompanied her brought her home against the blizzard, when every animal instinct would have prompted her to turn tail and drift with the wind. So Kit, for that was her name, became not only a pet but a family hero.

No one who has never lived on the early plains can conceive of those sudden storms. Down from the North they'd sweep, driving stinging pellets of icy snow straight before, wiping out all landmarks, making it even difficult to breathe and piling mountains of drifts over fence and field. There was nothing to break their force. The land was mostly open and unfenced. There was timber only along the streams, and even about the prairie homes there were no trees as yet, save a few struggling cottonwoods brought from the creek bank and kept alive by barrel after barrel of water poured at their feet. These same winds later were the scouring winds which swept naked the dust bowl; when avaricious mankind and foolish national advice, denuded the high plains to plant wheat killing the native grasses, and leaving the farms open to destruction.[5]

But I deviate from my tale. I started to speak of the old white mare "Kit" and ran off the track with other recollections.

It was a warm Sunday afternoon in early spring. Father had brought Kit around onto the front yard and let her nibble on the springing grass. I was four that February; and I felt myself quite grown up. So I began my plea to be allowed a ride. Kit was perfectly safe for any one. She had not an ounce of meanness in her any place. I would run about her and cling to her neck or fore leg with perfect impunity. So I got my permission. Father picked me up and sat me on Kit's back. I looked down and the ground seemed miles away. Father started leading my mount around the yard. I clung to the mane as tight as possible. But it was no use. In spite of my fright or perhaps because of it, I felt myself losing balance and suddenly I was lying on my back on the ground with Kit looking around at me in mild surprise, wondering what new style of horsemanship this was.

In spite of the early failure, my enthusiasm for riding was not dulled. It was only a few years later that I had my own horse and was riding everywhere. And I rode that horse without a saddle, seated Indian fashion on a folded blanket kept in place by a circingle, or belt around the horse.

The idea was that if I really wanted to be a proficient rider I must develop the grip of my legs so as to maintain my balance and have a seat that would be comfortable to both me and my mount. We did this for so long, that I was later able to ride for quite a time simply by holding the horse's sides with my knees, not touching either stirrup or saddle seat. I got my first saddle on my 14th birthday; but even after that it was frequently too much trouble to put it on and I'd take my seat bareback as before.

CHAPTER 4

We Take a Journey

It was fall in Kansas. If you have ever lived there or visited there in that season you will know what I mean, when I say there never, anywhere, were more perfect days. There is always a bit of sadness in the passing of summer. What in the dawn of the year we had planned and anticipated so often can be only partly accomplished; and we know the approaching days will be cold and unpleasant. It seems that in the plains states autumn tries her hardest to console us for what we have missed and reconcile us to what must come.

This is the season of the year when roads and hillsides are flaming shumac, woodlands aglow with the red of oak and yellow of maple and cottonwood. But why try to describe it when Professor Carruth of Kansas University did it so much better. In his words,

> A mist on the dim horizon, the infinite, tender sky,
> The rich brown tints of the cornfields
> And the wild geese winging high,
> And over the upland and lowland the glory of goldenrod.
> Some of us call it Autumn,
> Others call it God.[1]

And as you went along through the country you might well meet rows of farm wagons loaded with sorghum cane, journeying to the sorghum mill. For most every farmer always included a patch of cane in his crops to be sure of molasses for his cornbread, and for the ginger cookies, and for what was sometimes called "Long sweetnin" in contrast to brown sugar (we had no granulated sugar), which was locally called "short sweetnin." The cane mills were simple affairs, out in the open. A crusher was operated by horse power; the horse hitched to a long arm extending out somewhere about 15 feet from a gear wheel which was operated by the horse walking round and round in a never ending circle. The gear wheel activated the crusher rollers, between which the cane was fed, a stalk at a time. The juice ran off and was caught in a long pan, and from there on was heated to reduce and thicken and the greenish scum that rose to be skimmed off. When about as thick as light honey it was packed in jugs or other container and set aside for winter. One of our great sports was a taffy pull. Good way for boys and girls to spend an evening together, and for hand to touch hand, which was quite a thrill. In those days girls had not cheated themselves by making themselves playthings. Well, again I digress. We would take the sorghum molasses and boil it down to a candy stage, and then, hands slicked with butter two of us would take a lump of the mixture, which had cooled only a trifle. You wanted to move fast, and would too, without any prompting. The molasses was pulled out between the makers, and as it began to droop the ends were slapped together and it was pulled again. This was kept up until it began to sugar, and then it was cut into sticks and set aside to thoroughly cool. I don't know how I might feel now; but there was a day when I felt sorghum taffy was the ultimate in goodness. In another way, the cane was a great delicacy to me. To get the fresh stalk and peel off the hard outside skin and cut the inner core into chewing lengths. That was a natural sweet with its own special taste.

Well, came one of those falls and as usual that time of the year my father wanted to do some camping out. This year however was to be a bit different. My mother had a brother practicing dentistry in Parsons, a large town about a four days journey by wagon from Longton.[2]

It always amuses me to see the driving done in some of our television shows. Horses going at a dead run, up hill and down. How one would expect a buggy or wagon to hold together is beyond me. And the riders setting out on a trip at a gallop. No horse could have stood an hour of such handling; and any vehicle would have fallen to pieces about the third jump. Driving horses were usually driven at a trot and with slight intervals of rest could cover from twenty to thirty miles a day hitched to a carriage or twenty or less with a loaded wagon. A rider who was used to the trail did not want a fancy gated horse, they were too tiring. What was prized was a horse that would fox trot, a slow, easy shuffling trot that was easy on both the rider and the horse. I don't suppose that the fancy breeders have left a fox trotter in existence.[3]

Great preparation was made for our journey. A new wagon was brought home from the store, bows were fitted and set in place; a wagon cover was fastened over them and the bed was loaded with the necessaries for at least three days out of doors. Mother and father would sleep in the wagon, and as the days and nights were still warm, Bill and I would take our rest on a pallet under the wagon. Horse feed also was loaded, and as our buggy horses were a bit light for that work, father brought a special team. We hitched early for a quick start and were on our way before sun up. A short distance from home we had to ford the Elk River, which was quite a large stream. Right in the middle of the waters one of the new horses balked. And no amount of urging could make him pull another inch. Of all the faults of horseflesh this is the worst. Some horses seem to be naturally balky; some become so from abuse, from being put to a heavier load than they can pull and whipped when they fail; and in timbered country by being stumped. You have often heard the expression well I'm stumped haven't you? Well this is true fact. In driving over cleared land, sometimes the front of a wagon would pass over a stump that had been cut too high and the rear axle would catch and hold the wagon immovable. If the driver is too persistent and keeps urging his team after they know they are licked, it is nothing uncommon for one to give up, and never thereafter be willing to pull against a load of any consequence.

There was nothing for father to do but to step out on the wagon tongue and unhitch the balky animal and ride him back to town. I never knew how he was able to get it done so quickly, but in almost no time he was back with a new horse, and our team gave us no trouble thereafter.

There was nothing particular to remember about our trip to Parsons. All went well, the delightful weather continued; and we had a happy visit, of which I remember but little. But the journey back is another matter. We had been out only part of the first day, when there came upon us the early nasty, chill fall rains from which there was no escape. We simply had to slog on under the lowering sky and make a wet camp at nightfall. We all huddled in the wagon, like herring in a can, tried to eat cold food, and to sleep as motionless as possible so as to not disturb the others. Another danger was, that while the canvas shed water beautifully, if you happened to press your head against it, or any other object for that matter, a leak would at once start where the canvas was touched. So by and large we had a miserable night and after a miserable attempt at breakfast we broke camp and journeyed on. My father vowed solemnly that he'd find a house to sleep in before another nightfall. The sun came out and dried us off and the world looked bright again. Remember that houses were few and far between in those days. You could ride for hours and see no sign of human habitation, so we felt we might have to rough it another night, and looked forward to it with considerable annoyance.

We traveled well in spite of the softened ground, until about four in the afternoon the skies began to darken, and the wind rose and we had all the reason to expect another downpour. Then to our surprise on topping a hill, we saw in the valley below about a mile away a new house and a little distance from it a shed barn. No one was in the yard, but a thin trail of smoke rose from the chimney so we felt assured there was someone at home. We drove as rapidly as possible to the front of the house, there was no fence around it, and were greeted warmly by a pleasant appearing young farmer. Tow headed youngsters peered around him from the door and we could hear other childish voices from within. Father told him of our plight and asked for lodging, which was offered at once. Father told the man that we would be no trouble; that we could sleep in the shed, and that we had our own food, to which he sharply replied that any man who stopped at his place stayed in the house, ate his food, and shared his company, take it or leave it. Stopping overnight in this way was more or less a common practice, where distances were long and accommodations far between. Also the having of company could be quite a treat to the host, especially his wife and children, far as they were out on the lonely prairie.

And now after all this talking, comes the part for which I really told this tale.

Supper was soon ready and we were invited to sit down and partake. The table was made of planks laid across sawhorses, and the chairs were boxes and nail kegs. The house was almost bare of any furniture except homemade, but it was bright and clean as were the faces of the seven children who shared their food with us. The father sat at one end of the table, mother at the other with my parents, my brother and I at one side and the children of the house at the other. No excuse was made for the bareness of the house. The owner took pride in what he had accomplished. Simple and good. The fare was simple and good too. In two or three places along the table, within easy reach of the diner, were pans heaped full of steaming, crusty corn bread. At mother's place was a huge crock of buttermilk and at father's a like crock of sweet milk. Within reach were plates of fresh country butter. This may seem slim fare to you; but to anyone who is really hungry there is no finer dish than hot buttered cornbread and milk. We all fell to with ardor. One little boy would hold out his mug and say "Sweet milk pap" and another to the mother with "Buttermilk mam" and so through the evening meal until it all was eaten. During the meal my mother had to keep nudging me now and then to make me quit staring at methods wholly new to me.

We spent the night on pallets on the floors and rose refreshed to another meal of cornbread and butter, this time with coffee with cream so thick it would scarcely pour. After we had hooked up, father offered to pay the man and was sharply told that his hospitality was not for hire, but if we came that way again, not to fail to stop in and visit.

As we drove away, father said to my mother "Deedie, there is a family I am going to watch, just to see what could come out of such circumstances." This promise he kept and to our delight, by the time

I was grown man one of those boys was president of a large bank and another one a member of Congress.

I often enjoy telling this tale to the young men and women of to-day who wail about their lack of opportunity. After all, opportunity is made, not given.

The rest of the trip was uneventful, save that the afternoon of the day in, was spent in yet another fall rain, with mist blowing through the openings at the end of the cover, and trickling from rope ends and fretting the horses. Even my father's yellow Fish Brand slicker[4] couldn't turn the wet, and we all arrived home wet and discouraged, and vowing never again to take such a vacation. I must have felt differently at the time than I do now, for I remember telling my grandmother, who lived next door that I never again wanted such a trip. Now as I remember it, it was great fun. What a wonderful thing is the ability to forget. Thank God we have selective memories which hold and review to us the happy and pleasant times. How sad it would be if all the troubles were remembered as poignantly as the pleasant.

CHAPTER 5

Fun on the Farm

The early winter following our covered wagon trip, my father sold his store, and purchased a large ranch a few miles from town.

For that era the place was well improved. A log house of ample size was in excellent condition. This was built in what was called a "two pen" construction. That is a large square pen, or building of logs was put up, and then another of the same size was built at a distance of ten or fifteen feet from the other and a roof was put over it all, leaving a roofed passageway between the two pens. This passageway was called a "dog trot." Just why I never understood, unless it was because this shady spot was a particular favorite of the household dogs on a hot summer day. This house had been built of large trees and the pens were about twenty-four feet square, and it was built two stories high so that there was a large room up and down in each pen. These four large rooms had been divided, to provide a living room and kitchen in one, two bedrooms in the other pen and four upstairs bedrooms. My grandfather and grandmother, and my mother and father and we two boys with a colored girl helper occupied the house and for our simple needs and rather few furnishings we found ample space.[1]

At about fifty yards from the house was a large log barn. The house yard was surrounded by a dry stone wall[2] which was a constant nuisance as rabbits were always taking refuge among the crannies and the dogs were knocking over the stones trying to get them out. Elk River ran almost straight about a quarter of a mile north of our house and a large, ever flowing creek came in from the southeast running to the back of our house about 200 feet, the creek joining the river about a half mile east of our house. Back of the house there was a wide depression or slough which was flooded deeply in wet weather. At the point where the creek and river join stood the small, white country school. The road from town crossed the Elk near the schoolhouse and passed on west past our front door. Thus our buildings and the school were on what could be called a wet weather island.

It was shortly after we moved to the ranch that I passed my fifth birthday, when for me a wonderful thing happened.

Before this time I had dressed as all small boys under five were dressed, that is kilts, and a shirt and jacket, and with long hair like a girl's. At five I was supposed to be "breeched" that is to get into the short trousers which I would wear until I was thirteen. Long trousers were never used by boys under that age. With many sighs and tears my mother finally yielded to custom and cut off my long golden curls; and laid them tenderly away as keepsakes. I was half sorry they had been clipped when I saw how it saddened my mother. But such a new experience couldn't long be dimmed and soon I was as joyful as I had been in anticipation.

When father was negotiating the purchase of the ranch he had discovered a large deposit of an excellent brick-making clay, and he had it planned to have enough brick molded and burnt on the place to build both a house and a barn. At that time brick were handmade. The man who did the work mixed the clay, molded the brick in wooden molds, set them aside to dry and when dried built them into a pile above a huge pile of firewood, which was then "fired" and the brick baked.

To do this work we employed four molders and handlers early in the spring. They made enough brick for an eight-room house, and for a barn adequate to care for our horses and equipment. All summer long these men worked; and fed at our table, and the women of the family had the task of preparing the food. At last they were done. Dead timber had been felled and piled, and over the piles rose two huge heaps of sun dried brick. It was a time of general rejoicing. And that night came one of those sudden downpours. Out of the banks came the creek and the river. All of our land was flooded and where the piles of brick had stood rose two mounds of sticky yellow mud. The summer's work, the expenses and the makers' wages all melted and gone. With that setback there was no money left to start another project so we just stayed on in the old log home.

The area around our home and the immediate buildings was about twenty acres in extent. All this was heavily wooded and up and down the streams the ground was always covered with trees. Game was plentiful, and brother Bill who was now twelve decided to learn to hunt. Somewhere or other he got hold of a muzzle loading shot gun; and just to show how differently obedience was regarded by the children of that day, whenever Bill wanted to hunt he had to load the gun in the kitchen where mother could oversee the process. She was afraid to let him carry his powder ball and caps, so after he shot once, if he wanted to shoot again he had to tramp back home to reload. I don't quite see that sort of obedience now, and I am sure that Bill never cheated by hiding out some of his ammunition. He was, for his age, a fair marksman and we frequently had squirrel or duck to add to our regular menu.

Back of our house the creek on the near side, had an abrupt bank dropping twenty feet or more to a narrow shelf about two feet above normal water. This spot was at a slight bend in the creek and the water for some yards was from six to ten feet deep. As a result this made a sort of pool where fish would be quite plentiful. Brother Bill cut stair steps down this high bank to the shelf and made himself what for a young boy was an ideal fishing spot. But to my deep disappointment I was forbidden to follow. The water was so deep, that my mother feared I might miss my step and fall in and drown. But Bill supplied many a meal of red horse, sucker, cat and perch and now and then a misguided bass.

One thing that amuses me now as I said earlier, was the misconception of people nowadays of the character and nature of the cowhands. We had many on the ranch and I was just at the age to tag along and pester. Most of them would shoo me off; but one boy who was, as I remember it, about eighteen years of age was more considerate. In fact I think he rather enjoyed pranking with me. I remember one summer day when we were together and he was doing some work in the yard, I stayed close to him for a while, then went to my mother and inquired "Mama, what makes Charley smell so funny?" "Hush, don't let him hear you," she answered, "It's just that not all people like us take baths. Charley's just a bit careless, I guess." Rather a far cry from the wild and wooly dandy on the TV screen.

After the first flood that ruined our dreams of a brick home we watched the streams with careful eye. Our neighbors poo poohed the idea of another flood, assuring us there had been nothing like it in the preceding twenty years. And then the storm came.

It started with the sky turning a sickly green, and then darkening till daylight was almost blotted out. From our doorway we could hear the streams beginning to roar.

With past experience to urge us, my parents and grandparents soon prepared to get out. The horses and cattle were loosed from the barn so they could care for themselves. Father hitched a big team of mules we used in heavy farm work, to a three-seated light wagon. All the family got in save grandfather who went ahead riding Kit so as to be able to open the gates which led to the road. By the time the team was hitched and we were ready to start mother carried me to the wagon through water reaching almost to the hub of the wheels. We were worried about being able to cross the slough to get to higher ground, and we did barely make it, the water lapping at the wagon bed, and when grandfather followed us, Kit had to swim part of the way across. We went up the hill to the west of our ranch to a neighbor whose home stood about halfway up the hill. The house was built on two levels, the upper or main part level with the road, and a kitchen and dining room at a lower level down the hill. After supper in the dining room we went up stairs to the "sitting room" and were visiting and chatting, when we heard a resounding crash from down stairs. Peering down we could see that the water had risen enough to flood the two down stairs rooms and tip over the table with the supper dishes, some of which together with the furniture were floating merrily about the room as the water rose.

Well, all we could do was to hitch up again and with the neighbors now with us, drive further west to the top of the hill where flooding was impossible.

We escaped just in time, for in a few hours the house where we had stopped was there no more. We found shelter at the first ranch atop the hill, and the house was really running over with escapees. Most of us slept on pallets on the floor; and from my place, all night long I could hear the roaring of the streams, like continuous distant thunder.

When the water finally receded in a couple of days, and we were able to get back we found utter havoc. Not only was all our furniture soaked and some broken, but the whole house was filled a foot or more deep with mud, which stank to high heavens. The only thing we could do was to shovel out the mess and sort out what things were still usable and wash, and then shovel and wash and then shovel and wash some more.

CHAPTER 6

The Writing School

Any of you ever hear of such a thing as a writing school?

I doubt it. But in the days prior to the general use of a typewriter when all correspondence had to be by hand, to write a legible script was quite an accomplishment.

Even in large offices all matter had to be written by hand and if a copy was desired they were written in a special ink called copy ink. Copies were made then by using a permanently bound book of very thin blank paper. The letter or other paper to be copied was placed in the book under a blank sheet, and over the blank sheet was placed a cloth dipped in water and run through a roller wringer. The book was then closed and put in a press where it was pushed up with considerable force. This press was comprised of two metal plates, the top plate moveable and capable of being screwed down and when time had been given, and the press was opened and the original, slightly damp and wrinkled, had been removed the formerly blank sheet would have a very perfect copy. These books when filled, were indexed and placed in the office records.

At that time and even after typewriters came into general use, this wet copy was the only way a copy could be made. So there were two sorts of typewriter ribbons in use, one inked with "record" ink and the other with "copy" ink. As late as the last years of the first decade of the twentieth century copying was so little understood, and so little used, that in order to use a carbon copy in evidence, the lawyer offering the same was compelled to put an expert on the stand to prove how the carbon copy was obtained and how one could tell such a copy from the original by the blurring and easy rubbing out of a carbon copy. Then too, until the First World War a great many stenographers were men rather than women. All typewriters were blind, that is the paper was face down UNDER the [carriage] rather than face up over it. To see what he had written the typist had to swing up the whole carriage and peer under it. It was not until about nineteen fifteen that visible typewriters came into general use.[1]

Writing was taught in schools, and every grade, at least once a day would have its writing class. Each student had a copy book, with usually a row of model letters at the top, and some bit of religious philosophy or business or moral teaching which the student had to copy, many times over, then hand his book in for criticism and grading. Perhaps it will seem old fashioned, but when I see the books with "Run, John Run, See John Run! See Jane watch!" and other such bits of great significance, I can well understand the modern teenager's attitude toward life. After you had written "A good name is rather to be chosen than great riches"[2] fifty times or more, that thought would be stamped on your perception from that day onward.

But these lessons in the regular school did not suffice. So there grew up a class of itinerant teachers, men who had remarkable skill with a pen, who would go about from town to town and hold a night school in one of the higher grade school rooms. This school was usually for a two week duration, meeting every night from about seven to nine o'clock.

As I said, these teachers were men of high skill in chirography,[3] and in addition to their teaching would prepare calling cards for the ladies, dance cards, if there was a dance in the offing, or any other bit of fancy writing that was desired. Their pay for these jobs and the tuition paid by each pupil, usually five dollars for the two weeks, provided them with an ample income; quite a bit better than the average local teacher. Their productions while overly "fancy" were in the main gracefully and skillfully done. One of their tricks was to draw elaborate pictures at one[4] sweep of the pen, without lifting it from the surface of the paper. Frequent subjects were birds at rest and in flight, for the curves and smoothness of a bird's shape rendered it especially useful for such drawings.

Each student had to provide his own illumination, which was a wax candle, stuck into a homemade holder and set at the right upper corner of the school desk. With a candle burning brightly at each desk, the light was more than ample to people whose idea of a brilliant light was a coal oil lamp.

These teachers all used the Spencerian System, so called. This was a very graceful script, slanted to the right at about a fifteen degree angle. When done by a professional, this could be very clear and legible. And as further ornamentation, it was proper to shade the letters. For doing this even at that time the old timers preferred a goose quill pen, cut precisely to each individual's preferred shape. For this purpose a small knife, very sharp of edge was carried, hence the name "pen-knife" for any such small knife became common usage. Most of us however, were satisfied with a steel pen, of which there were three forms in general use: the "Stub," which was a very short, blunt point and was usually used for coarse writing and for rapidity, because, blunt as it was, the point would not stick into the paper which the other two sometimes did. The second was a "Falcon," shaped something like a spearhead, and was the point most in general use by men. The [third] was a "Spencerian," very fine of point, used for producing small letters and delicately shaped. This was frequently used to make entries in records where only a small space was allowed for the article or thing to be written. This was also the type of pen usually used by ladies in their personal correspondence. For in that as in all else the women desired to appear to be truly feminine.

The shading was produced by putting heavier pressure on the pen at any point where a thicker line was desired.

Attuned with the shaping of the letters, and the precision sought for, there was also a formality about the matter written. Certain phrases had an almost universal use. One such phrase, among the ladies was "With pleasure I take my pen in hand to inform you of ——." I know one letter of that sort which I saw in that time long past, which began with the rather gruesome statement "With pleasure I take my pen in hand to inform you of our dear mother's death."

After the Spencerian system was no longer in use came the era of the vertical, in which letters were all supposed to be completely erect, then came the "back hand" slanting the letter to the left, and finally what we now call writing with the letter slanted as though jumbled by a cyclone, and leaving more to the imagination than they impart of certain knowledge. For penmanship, like any other talent, unused will atrophy; and I am quite sure the days of beautifully written themes is that of the past.

These writing schools were not confined to young people; but were attended by old and young, for many of the older people had so little formal education that they seized upon any opportunity to improve themselves. It was no unusual thing to see parents, children, and grandparents attending the same class, and with some of the adults having a sad time of it trying to squeeze their ample proportions into the narrow space between seat and desk. These schools were my introduction to teaching outside the home; as I did not attend public school until my ninth year. My mother being a former school teacher, started me out and covered the first three grades at home. So these writing schools, which I was able to attend gave me some of the skills which I might not have otherwise received. But then our whole family attended, mother, father and brother Bill as well as I. And this was about the first time in my life that I became really aware of a girl. She was a little sprite of about my own age, and I verily believe the very last person in the United States or possibly the world to wear pantalets. If you don't know what these were, they were leg coverings, one for each leg, extending about three inches below the knee cap covered with ruffles, and with the top secured sometimes by elastic, sometimes by ties, under the skirt about halfway up the thigh. This of course I have only knowledge of at second hand.[5]

These events now bring us to a time we sought another home, of which more at a later time.

CHAPTER 7

New Scenes and Greener Pastures

There were a number of reasons which, combined, induced our removal from my birthplace. One of these arose from the prohibition amendment to the Kansas Constitution which had been recently adopted,[1] outlawing the saloon and prohibiting the sale of alcoholic beverages except for medicinal purposes upon the prescription of a licensed physician. My family were strongly in favor of the amendment and my father campaigned for it with all his energy and ability. This was contrary to the sentiment of a great majority of the people in this area at that time, and as a result my father's business suffered a sharp decline. In fact he and my grandfather were at a point where, if they cleaned up their business obligations little or nothing would be left. In addition to this was the matter of education for my brother and I.

Longton had only grade schools, with indifferent teaching quality. Several citizens, father included had tried to start and operate an academy, but that proved unsuccessful. High Schools were just coming into operation and were usually a one or two teacher affair, in a couple of rooms in the grade school building. Some fifty miles to the north of us was the town of Eureka, a county seat of good size, with good public schools, including a rather primitive high school. But it was also the home of the Southern Kansas Academy, a school maintained by the Congregational Church for the purpose of preparing leaders for the foreign mission field.[2]

This was the school which I finally attended and that it was successful in producing missionaries is attested by the fact that from my own graduating class three went into the foreign mission field. Two of them, Louis Fritz and his wife, served many years as missionaries in Iran and the third, a colored boy, served in Africa, and returning to the active ministry in this country, became finally Bishop John Gregg of the A.M.E. Church with his home in Kansas City, Kansas and a record of great and noble service as a great preacher, but also more than that as a leader of his own people. Many a young colored man in that area, will to this day, declare that he received his inspiration and at times material help from Bishop Gregg. So, although he is gone now, his influence is still a matter with which to take account.[3] Perhaps had more John Greggs been produced through the south there would be less turmoil today.[4]

So the remnants of the stock in trade of the store were traded for an equity in a rather poor prairie farm near Eureka, which my grandfather took over and operated, together with a scanty store of ancient farm tools and a few plug[5] horses. Like most German descended boys, my father had in his youth learned a trade. It was always considered best, that no matter what a man's vocation in life might be, he was best prepared to meet its dangers and perplexities if he had a good trade to fall back on in case of an emergency. So in his youth my father had become a very expert sheet metal worker. With grandfather and grandmother on the farm and in a place to care for their own needs, father secured a job as a sheet metal worker in a local store, and with five dollars in change his entire fortune, rented a house for his family, stored his tools and went to work.

This first job was a twelve-hour day, six day a week affair at the wage of two dollars and fifty cents a day. That seems utterly ridiculous today, but at that time was above average. Many unskilled workers were earning, and rearing a family, on as little as fifty cents per diem. And the hours were not too bad, when the merchant opened his doors at six thirty in the morning and usually kept them open until nine or after at night. It was in these long evenings that the chairs grouped around the cannon stove furnished a classroom for political and religious discussions almost every night. If you don't know what a cannon stove was, it was a huge, round affair, of a sort of bottle shape, standing over five feet high, and with a flat top on which there was usually a pot of coffee simmering. The stoves when fired up were capable of pouring out a tremendous volume of heat, capable of warming a long store room to a point where it was livable anywhere in it, but most cozy a few feet from the source of warmth. These stoves stood, usually over an open box about four feet square, filled with sand, which served not only to protect the floor from burning; but also was handy to receive the overflow from "chawin terbaccer" and pipe ashes. Cigarettes were unknown, and only the lawyer, doctor, and banker ever smoked cigars.

These stoves were especially desirable when they were in a general store where barrels of crackers, and pickles, and rounds of yellow cheese and other comestibles were handy. It was solid comfort for the villagers to sit about the stove, chairs tilted back against a barrel or counter if possible, and to indulge in lunch and argifying.[6] One of the special treats was to get the shallow lid off a hatbox and break into it a half dozen eggs and a big box of cove oysters, scramble them together and serve them hot to the group. An expert could do this by quick handling without more than slightly scorching the box lid.

The old country store—it was killed by specialized fancy groceries, saddle shops, hardware stores, clothing stores, etc. and was thought a thing of the past. I can still catch the aroma of kerosene, new harness, apples and vegetables, vinegar, and all the other items of the stock with an occasional interlarding of soft coal smoke! But gone forever? Not a bit of it. The supermarket of today, which we regard as something quite recent, is but a revival of the old general store, brought up to date, and deprived of its comfortable, homey atmosphere for one of efficiency and cold merchandising.

Father was never satisfied long to work for wages; and by rigid economy, within eighteen months had saved enough to start another business venture of his own. I don't suppose the tale of that venture would be of interest to you; but there are a few tales I might reveal of the business methods of that day.

The store was a small frame building, with a false front, a la Dodge City; the front two thirds devoted to new and used furniture. And I must confess that for the larger part of the stock was the used variety of rather questionable ancestry. The back room was a tin shop where the old set of tinner's tools found their proper place.

The tin smith in the eighties, was a far different business than that of today. All of the things done now were done then; but that was only a small part of the tin smith's product. In addition most household cooking utensils were hand made in the shop. Pans, wash boilers, tea kettles and the like were all carefully laid out, cut into pieces and assembled. Among one of the things in most demand in the summer were cans for canning vegetables and fruits. The Mason jar was unheard of. The cans were made in quart and half gallon sizes, with a top which fitted into a groove[7] on the can and into which hot sealing wax was poured and allowed to harden. This wax was a product largely composed of resin, and in the heating process to prepare for the sealing gave off a pleasant piney smell and all summer long, going down the town streets you could tell where fruit was being canned by the aroma of the melting wax. When the season was at its height, the work would begin as early as it was possible to see and continue until far into the night. Fruit kept in these cans was fresh and wholesome when taken from the cellar shelves. At first the tinner made the entire can top and bottom, but after a few years ready made tops and bottoms were on the market which made the making of the can a simpler and easier matter. Another use for the half gallon cans was to solder a loop of tin about two thirds of the way from the top, solder the top in place so the can would be airtight, slipping a strap through the loops and trapping it to one's back as a water wing. They worked beautifully and a young swimmer was perfectly safe with them, unless he tried an experiment which I tried once, and strapped them to his feet. My feet went up and my head went down and I well nigh drowned myself before I could get myself loose. The expert tinsmith was able to obtain a description and measurement of any vessel desired, and then take a compass and try square[8] and mark the pieces out on a sheet of tin, cut them out and produce the exact vessel required. The sheet tin was much heavier and more durable than anything found today and a well-made pan would last for many years.

In addition to the shop work there was always waiting, a flat roof to be covered with sheets of tin, soldered at the seams and nailed down. If kept painted such a roof would last for years. But if anyone ever wished to get a first rate idea of Tophet[9] let him try putting on a tin roof in the middle of August with a hundred degree Kansas sun so intense that the glaring sheets of tin would scorch a cloth dropped on them and left too long. I know all this because I sometimes helped in rush times in the shop and on the roof too. One great thing about such a tin roof I found in the one that covered my bedroom; to hear the singing of the summer rain or the rattling of winter sleet and curl up in my bed in complete security. Another product of the shop were candle molds, candle sticks, and lanterns. The lanterns were just a perforated tin box with a bail on top, a door where a candle could be inserted in a candle stick inside. Lighted, these made a fair light and didn't blow out. The candle molds were shaped to insert a string or rag for the molded variety. The other way candles were made were "dips." A string was dipped into a pot of melted wax, or fat, tallow preferred, drawn up, and hung on a line and as soon as hardened partially, re-dipped and re-hung until the film of tallow added at each dip brought the candle to the desired size.

Father's store was on the Main Street, just across the street from the Court House Square. Main Street was a wide street and of course as all town streets at the time, wholly unpaved. At each crossing were cross walks of stone a little higher than the street level and reaching from wooden sidewalk to wooden sidewalk. Of course in the summer these streets would be a desert of powdery dust and in rainy or winter weather, when not frozen would be a sea of goo almost knee deep or hub deep to the horses, and every horse step came with a sucking plop. Kansas already had a marriage license law,[10] and couples coming in frequently tied their horses to a hitch rack in front of father's store, and we would get a view of their coming and going for their license.

One day in early spring, when the ground had thawed and the moisture of winter snows had turned the surface into a lake of slop about as thick as a thin gravy, one such young couple came in and hitched. The young man was dressed uncomfortably in his Sunday's best and the bride to be was all frilly, long white dress, big straw hat with a stuffed bird perched, precariously, on top, white gloves, and as she got out of the wagon one could catch a flash of long white cotton stockings, and high buttoned patent leather shoes. She was carefully piloted across the street and from the time it took for their return we well knew they had lingered to have the probate judge tie the knot. As they came across the street the groom this time marched proudly ahead, and the bride meekly followed. The groom untied the team and climbed up to the wagon seat and waited for his lady love to scramble aloft as best she could. Just as she was in the act of stepping from the wagon wheel hub to the step on the side of the wagon bed, the team made a sudden lurch, and down she went, flat on her back in the mud which engulfed her almost completely. Never had a marriage started out more unpropitiously. She shook herself, wiped the mud out of her eyes, shook as much [as] possible out of her hair and off her battered finery; then climbed aboard, and we could see them as they plodded down the road, she shaking her finger and the groom shivering as far across the wagon seat as he could get.

Those were hard days for the Kansas farmer. Prices for farm products when there was any market at all, were disastrously low. Corn went begging at ten cents a bushel, wheat was often around forty cents or lower. The livestock, cattle and hogs were only a few cents a pound. You could buy enough steak for a dime to feed a family of five. Eggs were a nickel a dozen. Bread was five cents a loaf and milk a nickel a quart.

Not that many people bought milk. Most families had one or two cows of their own. But what was sold, came to town in twenty-gallon cans. The customer met the milk wagon with a pitcher or small tin pail, and the milkman ladled out the required amount with a long handled ladle holding a quart. Sanitation was unheard of. Just why one never was afflicted with a myriad of communicable diseases, is hard to understand.

But even with these low prices, many farmers were unable to survive. The rosy pictures painted by the land companies were only pretty on paper. The reality of the sod house, the desolate treeless prairie, the monotony and hardship, the disappointment when they tried to sell their crops, and often had to haul them back to the farm for want of any market at all, broke the heart of many a settler. It was nothing unusual to see a farmer come to town, with all his goods loaded into his farm wagon, with all his family, leading a cow or two, perhaps with a crate of chickens alongside, and sell the whole outfit for train fare back home in the east. And the merchant who bought these goods seldom made much on them, for he had as hard a time to dispose of them as had the farmer. It took real men and women to brave such rigors. As a matter of fact I have seen my own grandfather haul a load of ear corn to town, and being unable to sell it, take it back home and burn it in the kitchen stove in place of the purchased coal. Farmers, now-a-days who complain of the profit made by the "middle man," who from the way the name is mentioned must be a son of Belial[11] fail to realize what it would mean to be as that time we were, without any middle man or anyone else to sell to. At least at the present time there is a market. I know of one very bad year when corn was down to a few cents a bushel, one enterprising man built long slat sheds on the right of way of the railroad,[12] shed after shed, and filled them with the cheap corn, and a couple of years later sold it at close to a thousand per cent profit.[13]

I know these tales are jumbled as to time of the occurrence; but I am more interested in picturing an era than I am in strict chronological order. One event happened in the fall of the year eighteen ninety-two that might be worth recounting. In my boyhood I was in a way blessed with two homes. My mother had an only sister, wife of a physician, living in Kansas City. They were childless, and I was always more or less a member of their household when it suited my fancy. That was the year of the second Cleveland-Harrison campaign for the presidency and I happened to be in Kansas City at the time of a grand Cleveland celebration. The President was to be present and to take part in a grand parade. The struggle between Harrison and Cleveland had been sharp for years. Cleveland was first elected following Chester A. Arthur; and was defeated at the end of his first term by Benjamin Harrison. Now at the end of the Harrison term he was fighting for a comeback. History will tell you he did the remarkable thing of replacing the man who unseated him. But that day in early autumn all was uncertainty. The town was in uproar. Jackson County, where Kansas City is located, had always been overwhelmingly Democratic as she still is. The streets were crowded, the horse cars hauling overflow loads, hackney coaches[14] bustling everywhere, and banners were waving from every available place. To a nine-year-old from the country, this was a fairy land. The parade was to be held at night to allow the usual torch light procession. Soon after dark we could hear the bands blaring, and I rushed to the window to see it all. First there came mounted police, then a band, then hundreds of marchers, walking two abreast, each man holding a blazing smoking torch, then more bands and more marchers, and on and on, and finally an open carriage and standing up, waving his tall silk hat, was the President himself. That picture will never fade or grow dim. I can still see the heavy, but erect, mustachioed president, and feel the attraction of his personality and dignity, even to a small boy.[15]

Another thing happened in the same city, possibly a few years earlier.

Kansas City had built, on the order of the Crystal Palace in London[16] a building which was called the Exposition Hall, and every year there was held there what was really an overgrown country fair. This building was wholly of glass, and shaped somewhat like a Quonset hut.[17] It was long enough to hold large exhibits and many many people. It stood in its place long after the fairs were a thing of the past, until it was sadly vandalized and had to be torn down. There was a large stage at one end, erected at a height of about ten feet from the floor, and on this were musicians and entertainers of various sorts. The day that I specially remember we were all enjoying band concerts by Pat Gilmore's band; the top ranking band of the nation. I was near the stage at the end of one number, when the conductor approached the stage railing asking for quiet, and announcing a solo by the band's first cornetist. A rather small, very slender young man stepped forward, and after a short prelude by the band started playing. Despite the fact that the hall was packed, that men were moving about, bargaining, and displaying their wares, suddenly all were silent and still. The silver tones rang with a lilt of triumph. In my memory this was one of the most beautiful instrumental offerings I ever heard. A day or two later I learned the name of the young soloist. It was John Philip Sousa, who after Gilmore's death took over the band as director; and everyone knows the rest of that story.[18]

At that time Kansas City was in many respects small town like. But few of its streets were paved. Transportation was by horse-drawn streetcars and hacks. There were ordinances fixing the number who could crowd on a horse car so as to not over tax the team; but these ordinances were constantly defied by people in a hurry to go somewhere or a driver anxious to swell his receipts. As a result every now and then a car would be stopped and the driver hauled off to the police station. The population of the city was approximately a hundred thousand. Our home was at the foot of a steep hill that the horse cars had to climb for a distance of about three blocks to turn around at the end. This hill was so steep that the car company had to keep extra teams at the foot of the hill to be hitched on ahead of the regular team and drag the car up the hill. Frequently I would sit at the window to watch this operation, and even then felt outraged at some of the treatment I saw given the horses. It was especially bad in slippery weather, when the drivers would whip the horses up the hill using a long cutting black snake whip when a few extra handfuls of oats under their skinny hides would have proved much better. Fortunately it was not long until the cable cars replaced the horse drawn. I must tell you about these cable cars. Down, underground, beneath an open slot running midway between the streetcar rails ran a never-ending cable, which received its energy from a powerhouse, and was kept moving all during the day. The streetcars were in a train, with an open grip car, ahead, and drawing a closed car behind it. Seats in the grip car were very popular in the summer but in cold weather the closed car with its coal burning stove won out. In a boxed off place in the middle of the grip car stood the Gripman. His duties were to operate a long mechanism which ran from the grip car down through the grip slot. By this he could take hold of the cable and the car would be carried along at whatever speed the cable was moving. To stop he released the grip and spun the hand brakes. This is the same device that exists now in San Francisco. Along the outer side of the grip car ran an entrance step on each side. No one was supposed to ride on this step; but that was another rule not too much enforced. Tickets were taken up or fares paid to a conductor who operated from the rear of the closed car, and who made trips to the front when new passengers were taken aboard. There is a steep hill in Kansas City, running a block on Ninth Street from Main to Walnut. It was a delight to small and active boys to "hop" the step on the grip car at the foot of this hill and drop off at Walnut before a fare could be called for; walk down hill to Main and repeat the performance again. At that time we were deadly afraid of the conductor, and he did catch one or two at infrequent intervals; but they never got more than a lecture about the danger of falling under the wheels. Now as I look back, I can see the man was more concerned for our safety than he was for the loss of a fare, which was only a nickel to any part of town anyway.

You could tell on what lines the cars went by the color of a stripe running around just under the eaves of each car. Yellow went out Troost, way way out into the country to Troost Park, ending at what is now Linwood Boulevard. Green went out Eighth past the home where I was now staying. It was such a pretty little brick bungalow standing on a gentle terrace. I saw it a few years ago and it was the office of a junkyard, and all about it where I had played, were piles of broken machines and the odds and ends natural to such a place. The beautiful and stately elms along Forrest Avenue were all things of the past.

There is one more thing that sticks in my memory. The grip car was equipped with a gong atop, with a cord in reach of the Gripman. He would ring this bell to announce his approach and as a warning to traffic. Ordinarily this bell gave a loud, clear ring. But in winter in a snowstorm, snow would pile up on it and muffle it. I can still go to the front window of my memory and see the headlight of the cars coming, through the driving snow and hear the "Clank, clank" of the muffled bell.

The streets in the winter were beautiful to me. Everyone drove horses and when the snow came you could hear the ringing of the bells on the horses drawing the cutters[19] which had replaced the buggies and carriages. In the summertime, Fifteenth Street, which they now call Truman Road, was a popular place for recreation. It was at that time a very wide, dirt road; and Sunday afternoons all the young swains would get the best livery rig[20] possible if they didn't have one of their own, take their best girl aboard and go to the neighborhood of Troost Avenue, and race the other drivers along Fifteenth eastward.

But it's time to get back home from Kansas City and tell you more of the Eureka days, which is what I started out to do.

CHAPTER 8

The Shape of Things in Little Things

The destinies of a man and of a culture are not, as a usual thing made up of world-shaking events. They are more like the course of a stream of water, rising from a small spring, and flowing onward, increasing in size, till, all at once we discover we are dealing with a wide river, which seems to have sprung magically into being. So in human life, the small event starts a trend that leads inevitably to a second and so on to the ultimate. Freedom of choice seems sometimes hard to accept when we can trace back along the course of history from event to event, and see how very little choice there was oft times involved.

So in trying to bring before you a picture of the times of my boyhood, I am perforce compelled to tell the little, common, daily happenings; which are so typical of the days of my youth. During my grade school years there was very little that occurred which I remember well enough, or which seems important enough to transcribe. But in the fall of the year 1894 I started my studies in the academy.[1]

Eureka, and the area around about it were made up of two, distinct ethnic groups. The river and the creek bottom farms, by the way about all the land that was really tillable, was owned by settlers of Swedish and Norwegian blood. They were the most wonderful, thrifty, kindly, neighborly folk imaginable. And I remember my days when I visited their homes with continuing delight. These farmers were the ones who winter fed cattle on grain. The upland ranches were settled largely by people from the middle states, Maryland, Kentucky, Tennessee, and some Missouri. The ranches were large in size, and the ranch houses as modern as the times permitted. But nearly all of the ranchers had good homes in town where they lived during the school season so that their children could attend the town schools. So my playmates at school were largely the children of the ranchers and business people of the town. Naturally we thought and talked cattle. One of my ways of getting to Kansas City was to take advantage of a Kansas law which required a cattle shipper to ship an attendant with every car in a cattle train. These attendants were supposed to see that the train was stopped at proper intervals and the cattle watered.[2] On a long distance ride this could be very necessary. For one of the slick tricks of some shippers was to starve their cattle of water, and then in the stock pens just before they were sold and weighed let them fill up with a hundred pounds or so of water, and sell the water at meat prices. Since Eureka was only about eight hours ride from Kansas City there was nothing for an attendant to do but ride along and fulfill the law so as to keep the shipper out of trouble. If I wanted a trip I'd pick out a shipment, get assigned to a car, get into the caboose and sleep until we pulled into the stockyards; then get my papers signed, and be done and have a ten day stay, to ride back home on the regular passenger train, all for free.

When was there a time when horse racing was not an intoxicating sport? At the present time we complain about the young car driver's craze for speed; but let me tell you, if my saddle pony hadn't been able to beat or keep up with the other boys' saddle ponies, I wouldn't have kept it longer than it took me to find a sale. I never had to worry about my driving horse for Don could out trot anything in that area. And he was too proud ever to let any one pass him on the road. Let some one try to pass he'd clamp the bit in his teeth and pull the buggy by the reins, while the harness tugs hung limp and useless. The town had a circular racetrack in a large meadow where county fairs were at times held. And the young men were there trying out their mounts with great frequency.

One use for this track was for another kind of race. There were in those days, itinerant jockeys, who'd drive about the country in a racing cart, driving one horse and leading another, and when they'd hit a town would get up a crowd of local sports and promote a race with some local horse. Their revenue came from bets on their steed and that horse could usually beat any local favorite. There was one exception however. In those days, groceries were delivered to your door. There was no cash and carry foolishness. And each grocery had one or two delivery wagons. At one store there was one of the most dejected, flea-infested bits of horsehide you could imagine. Whenever one of these traveling horsemen came along and left word he'd be at the fair grounds track to meet all comers, the delivery boy would drive down there in the delivery wagon, and stand his old plug, untied. To see it standing there, hip sunk, head dangling and ears flopping at the end of a scrawny neck was to seem to be looking at a scare crow. After much persuasion and joking and laughing, a stiff bet at fine odds for the locals would be worked up with the out of towner against old Whitey. Then came the transformation. Out of the harness, with only a bridle, the head came up, the eyes rolled, the nostrils flared and when they went to the line with the driver riding Whitey bare back, we all knew what would happen. I think the other party guessed it too, for one could frequently read with amusement the utter astonishment with which he saw his foe. And at the word go away they went, with Whitey ahead from the start. He'd come in under wraps, go back into his working clothes, and stand again, the picture of dejection while his master and the other boys collected the winnings. There were too many local people on hand to permit the outsider to try to renege. This happened time after time, until Eureka grew to be avoided by the traveling horsemen like a pestilence. If any came that way, he drove straight on through without a pause.

Speaking of horses, I had another mount for a couple of years. When father brought him home we were amused and rather taken a-back at the same time. Where father ever found him is beyond my comprehension. For he was one of the true Appaloocians;[3] and there never was an uglier animal. The so called Appaloosa horses which have become quite popular of late are nothing but very ordinary quarter horses bred with just enough Appaloosa blood to give them the skin and hair coloration especially notable in that breed. The genuine Appaloosa was bred by the Nez Perce Indians as a war horse. They developed unusual staying powers, with all the gentleness and intelligence of their pure Arab forefathers. But in place of being round and smooth, the genuine article was rugged and unshapely. The withers were unusually high, the hips sloped sharply downward to end in a tail that looked like it had been hair cut to, almost no hair by a very careless barber. The neck was long and thin and ended in a bony head, it was almost devoid of any mane. Two huge ears, flopped almost as large as a mule's. The iris of the eye was very small and the eye rolling white like the animal was in a perpetual state of terror. And his coloration, which was a natural camouflage, was striking. The skin about the muzzle and the eyes was a sickly pinkish white. The forequarters were usually roan, and the rest of the animal spotted and dappled in some spaces to look like a spotted saddle blanket; at others just a splash of colour here and there on a background resembling the colour of the four quarters. The legs were clean and strong, ending in about as incongruously huge a set of hoofs as could be imagined. But this ridiculous shape was one of his virtues. The sloping hips gave him an immense leverage for a quick, jumping start, and the huge hoofs added traction and ability to travel over rough ground where a smaller hoof would tend to turn and strain the legs.[4]

Added to all of this Bob, for that was this fellow's name, had at some time been entangled in barbed wire, and had about cut off his head, and had a huge scar running almost completely around his neck at the largest part next to the withers. Father used this horse for his business trips to the country. Mother would never ride in public behind such a looking beast. So it was my task whenever she wanted to visit, to have me take her phaeton[5] and my Don and acting as coachman, carry her on her rides.

In spite of all appearances I sometimes took Bob for use under the saddle. He had a delightful, easy lope that he could keep on for hours. In fact one of my ranch friends with whom I visited in the summer, lived seventeen miles from Eureka, and I'd put Bob at a canter when I left home, and he'd never break that canter, save to change leads, until I rode up to my friend's gate. And he'd be breathing smooth and

A. J. Bolinger feeds chickens, circa 1890s. (Photograph courtesy of Mary Margaret Concannon)

natural at the end. One reason I'd like to ride Bob on this particular trip, was that there was a wide river that had to be forded. For some reason every time I'd cross this ford on Millie she'd wait until the deepest part, and then without warning lie down. I didn't much like this for when she did that and the water suddenly engulfed me up to my armpits it was rather disconcerting. She'd get up, shake herself like a dog and go unconcernedly on her way. But in chilly weather this could be a very unpleasant experience.

The Southern Kansas Academy was an institution well worthy of the fine reputation it bore.

The town of Eureka sits in a bend of Fall River, which comes from the north, along the west side of the town, then curves around the south and part of the east side. Main street ran from the river due north to end in a quite appreciable hill, and the academy was perched atop that hill. It was a large brick, stone trimmed building with a central clock tower facing Main Street, and it stood about an even mile from the south end of main.[6] There were approximately ten acres in the campus, and on them were a football field, a baseball diamond and several tennis courts. Football had just begun to assume its present form; prior to this time in all the grade schools there was played a species of Rugby, which is just now coming back into public favor after an eclipse of nearly three-quarters of a century.

The faculty of this school was carefully selected and fully competent. In fact it was here that I met the man who was, to a greater extent than [any] other to influence my after thinking, and to imbue in me much of my feeling of respect for man's integrity, and our duty to recognize his worth. This man, Scroggs, was a surprising character. Built in rather a Falstaffian way there was perched on a short neck a very round head, large in size, and crowned by a fringe of disheveled red hair around a large bald forehead. The face was partially concealed by a shaggy red beard, carelessly trimmed enough to keep it out of his way. His arms were short and his hands large and stubby. To see those hands flying over the keyboard of a piano was a continuing surprise. His fondness for music was intense, and before he had been Principal of the academy for many days he had glee clubs going among both boys and girls, whose work together is still a pleasant memory. This man, after he finished at S.K.A., became a teacher and later president of Oklahoma University, and his record as a teacher and leader stood out there as it had in the small school with us. One of his favorite comparisons was to say, "You know all fish have bones; but you don't eat the fish for the bones, but for the meat. You don't say to a guest, look what lovely bones this fish we are having, has. You'd say, eat the fish and push the bones aside. So it is with your fellow man. All men have faults, some big and some little, some many and some few, but like the bones in the fish, don't strangle over the faults, push them aside and enjoy the meat of his good qualities."[7]

On some of my trips to Kansas City I had complained about repeated headaches. These had bothered me since my first school days. That summer, when I was eleven, I was complaining again and more than ever. The idea of corrective glasses for youngsters was just beginning to be advanced, and a few medical practitioners had done some special study, and set themselves up as oculists. This time my uncle decided that the possibility of an eye defect should be looked into, and so took me to one of such practitioners. His verdict was that I was terrifically astigmatic and should be wearing glasses during all my waking hours. I was fitted at once, and the correctness of his diagnosis was disclosed by my never having one of my headaches after that day. But my spectacle wearing had another effect. The only contact the average man or woman of that day had with any eye treatment was with the traveling spectacle vendor, who went about the country with a valise full of glasses, all frames and lenses complete, and fitted his patient by trying on one set after another until one was found that rendered the best results. To these good folks, spectacles went only with age and fading sight. When I, a boy of eleven, went on the street I was for many weeks an object of wonder. This finally wore off but I was stuck with a nickname that stayed with me from that day on until I left Eureka after my graduation from the Academy. I was "Speck" Bolinger from that day on.

"Hay Speck! Come on. Billy Morris has bought a contraption that they call a 'safety bike,' and he's going to learn to ride. Come on, let's see." Such a challenge from one of my friends told of the coming to Eureka of the first of our present models of bicycles. Billy Morris was owner of one of our local drug stores, and was always inclined to grab anything new he could learn about. This time he had beat them all.

Up to this time all our bicycles were the high wheel type, one big wheel in front and one small wheel at the end of a long frame behind, with the rider's seat perched directly over the axle of the front wheel. I had one and knew all about them. You can see such an affair used now frequently in circus acts. They weren't too bad going uphill, but perched as you were, immediately over the center of gravity, start downhill and if the front wheel struck a stone or rut and you weren't lightning quick to lean backward, the front wheel would come directly to a stop, and the hind wheel and frame, with you on top, would revolve gracefully on the front axle, and project you ahead like you were shot from a catapult.

This new contraption which our druggist had acquired had two equal size wheels, like the present day machine; but these wheels were equipped with hard rubber tires. The hind wheel was operated by an open chain drive, so that the rider had to don short trousers and long stockings or be in danger of grinding the right leg of his trousers in the sprocket wheel. Mr. Morris was a short man, perhaps five foot four or five, and had a long Billy goat whisker. He had quite a gallery that first night, when he took his first ride. After many a false start he took off down the road, with his Derby hat clamped firmly to his head, and his whiskers and coattail flying in perfect harmony. He wobbled and twisted and generally made a bad time of it, but with much ribald advice he finally got the hang of the thing, and in a few days was riding about town with great confidence and to the envy of all beholders.

It was only a few years until someone had thought of air filled tires, which at first were equipped with tube and the whole had to be dismounted and taken apart and the inner tube patched, when one of the frequent punctures occurred.

But the traveling spectacle salesman was not the only regular visitor. The umbrella mender was also a regular. He usually combined knife and scissors sharpening with his umbrella mending. He would repair any part of an umbrella from fastening the cover when it broke loose, or replacing a broken rib, even putting on a whole new cover. When everyone was thrifty and saved and repaired household equipment, and when nearly everyone, men included carried an umbrella as a protection from the rain, and also on very hot days, you can see where one might develop quite a clientele.[8]

Then too there was the Italian with his trained bear, who gathered a group of children about him and had the bear dance or wrestle for the pennies and nickels that might be tossed to him. There was also a group of kilted Scots who made their way about giving screeching bag-pipe concerts. Entertainment was simple but adequate.

And when you add in the patent medicine shows, some with a primitive set of carnival rides, always including a merry-go-round, you had really something!

One of these that we always loved to see come to town was the one peddling Harlan's Wizzard Oil; a rare specific, for internal or external use as desired and applicable to almost any disorder known to man.[9] Also there was one calling itself "The Arms of Tilly" and purporting to be one handled by the family of the great German general of that name. I remember it was advertised by a banner proclaiming its motto as "MEDICAMENTUM DEUS PROBATUM."[10] All very awe inspiring to a public to whom Latin meant learning and verity per se.[11]

The usual set up [was] in a vacant lot on Main Street. There would be one or more beautiful wagons or caravans, at the back end of one [of] which was a large tail gate which could be let down to furnish a stage. The banjo picking black face comedian was always a wonder of wit. The dialogues between him and the "Doctor" were great to hear. And we didn't mind the periods set to peddling their nostrums too much, for it was always fun to see who would be first to crowd up and spend a dollar, the customary price, for a remedy that would protect them from all future ills. Then the next night you could be sure that one or more of these first night purchasers would appear to give testimony as to the wonderful effect even a couple of doses had had upon their various complaints.

I believe I was talking about the academy. I wonder how I got to wandering off in this way. Well, our minds play tricks on us, and calling up one scene will eventually bring up a score of others.

The Swedish and Norwegian farmers up and down the river and creek valleys, were among our most prosperous and forward-looking citizens. Many of their older children attended the academy with me and I was always delighted when I got an invitation to come to one of their homes for a meal. It was always delightfully old world in many of its dishes, but the environment itself was added pleasure. The homes were always immaculately clean, the colours were bright and crisp, the parents big, laughing, merry folk.

It was here that I got my introduction to stock fish. Having a large clientele who demanded it, every grocery carried a supply of these fish. They were about 30 inches long, dried hard as a rock and bound in bales with wire. The bales were about three feet in diameter and stood on end, were scattered about the store, or even allowed to stand outside the store, on the front walk. This was hardly an extremely sanitary way of handling them, but no one ever seemed to suffer from it. Perhaps those farmers were just too healthy and active for any germ to dare attack them.

The farm women would take these stock fish and soak them in a lye solution, and then run water over them, in a long and intricate process of preparation, and when done they were really quite good.

But then all food was simple and nourishing. Diets were balanced until one would need have no worry about a vitamin deficiency or a deficiency of any other kind.[12]

The average breakfast would be one of fried or poached eggs, ham or bacon, hot bread, coffee with clotted cream, hot oatmeal or cornmeal mush, varied sometimes with creamed chipped beef, and in winter always on hand buckwheat cakes, with loads of sweet butter and maple syrup; real maple syrup. We got huge blocks of pure maple sugar, and shaved that and made our own syrup. Also there was frequently cod fish, either in potato balls or chipped and creamed. It was a meal for a working man. The noon lunch would figure a roast, a baked chicken or other fowl, fried ham or other meat, a homemade bread, a home canned vegetable or two, potatoes, baked, boiled, or mashed, fruit, jelly, pickles and pie. The supper was usually cold cuts, country fried potatoes cornbread or corn dodgers, a cake made of corn meal, salt and water and baked until crisp and brown, light bread, and anything that was on hand left from another meal.

No one ever left a table hungry. That wasn't at the time the proper thing to do. Perhaps their lives were shortened a bit, but they enjoyed the shortening process.

There was one thing in these Scandinavian homes which always interested me. When we sat down at the table, only the men took their places. My little friend (if a girl had invited me) stood behind my chair, as the other women folk behind the chairs of the other men, and saw that our plates were never empty, until we could eat no more. Then the men left the table for a moment's snooze, in a chair, on a couch, or simply stretched out on the floor, and the women had their meal. I often remarked at this custom and was informed that the women wouldn't want it any other way. They could get the men folk filled up and out of the way, eat their own meal at their leisure, visit with one another, and then be ready to clean up after the meal without anyone around to bother them.

These Swedish women were wonderful cooks; but it wasn't confined to the women alone. At that time every town had its bake shop. Bread wagons and big bread concerns were unknown. And in Eureka the bakery was run by a Swede. All his wares were good, but my memory clings to a hearth loaf of pure rye. This bread was shaped into round loaves about 10 inches across and baked outside the oven on the hearth. When the weekly batch was baking, if the windows of the shop were open, you could smell the hot fragrance of the rye with its mixture of carroway seeds [a] block away.

One of the best memories of a Swedish farm home comes from a springtime dinner which was given for our whole class.

It was 1899, the year of our graduation, so all of us felt very mature and self sufficient, looking at the world as our opportunity for action, with great anticipation; and yet with a bit of fear too, at giving up the known ways for the new.

Since the evenings in late May in Kansas are normally fine, it was decided that the twenty class members would have a hay ride the ten miles out to the farm, have our dinner, or rather as we called it our supper, and then enjoy a ride back home.

I doubt very much if any teenager today can experience the thrill of that ride. The frames for hauling hay were wide affairs fitted to the wagon running gear after the bed had been removed. The bottom was below the top of the rear wheels, and to compensate for this and permit a wider platform there was a raised hood, or housing or perhaps fender over the rear wheels. Over this was spread about eighteen inches of clean new hay, blankets were scattered about and the crowd climbed in and settled down on the sweet smelling hay. And really there is no perfume ever half as sweet as the breath of clean, new hay. And what a time that was for secret hand touchings, for moving closer together, and all the other timid overtures of love which the [illegible word] of the time might wink at but must never openly know.

Many of the class had in their last couple of years in the academy, done what would now-a-days be called dating; though then it was a much more limited thing than that designation now implies. We expected to have supper about seven, and as there was a bright moon shining, there would be no difficulty in making the return trip.

All started out beautifully. We rode along the gentle country lanes, singing and laughing and talking, and then all at once the iron tire on one of the rear wheels rolled off.

These tires were not bolted in any way. When one was put on a wheel it was "set" to the wood by heat. Under ordinary circumstances this would make a grip that was almost impossible to remove intentionally. The tire was heated red hot, a section of it was put in a "crimper" which by use of a long lever handle squeezed a section of the tire in on itself and so reduced the diameter; then the tire, while still hot, was forced on the wooden wheel and immediately cooled off with water. As a result the tire in cooling would shrink and remain fast to the wheel. But there was one difficulty. In dry weather the wooden wheel would sometimes dry out and loosen its hold on the rim, and as a result would run off the wheel in traveling. The vehicle was then out of service, for to have driven it even a short distance without the tire would have caused the wooden wheel to collapse. So there was nothing for us to do but replace the rim and find some way of binding it on.

Looking about the place nothing could be found but a few pieces of rusty barbed wire fencing. After this had been broken into usable lengths it was wrapped about the tire and the wooden rim of the wheel and twisted into [place]. We all drew a sigh of relief and climbed back in and I resumed my seat on the wooden fender over the wheel. This fender was not a solid affair but was made of wooden slats about an inch apart. We were glad to be off, for we had gone only about half the way, and there was a cloud sidling up toward the face of the moon.

Then, it happened.

My perch was directly above the wheel that had lost its tire and the boys who had wrapped that wire hadn't done too good a job. In the stress of travel it worked loose and an end came up through one of the cracks in the fender and caught my best Sunday britches right at the top of the seat, and with a strong downward pull, tore a chunk of the seat about five inches square. Knowing nothing better to do I slid from the fender, down into the hay and there remained.

But the worst was not yet.

The cloud which had slowly been creeping up, now took wings and raced to obliterate the moon. Rain began to fall in sheets. We had nothing for protection but a few blankets which we gallantly, if a bit reluctantly, surrendered to the girls.

Our host's home was near at hand, but there was a river to cross, with a high bank on the opposite side nearest the house. When we made it across the rapidly rising river, the opposite bank was so slippery that the team couldn't pull the loaded wagon to the top, so there was nothing for us to do but to drive as closely to dry land as we could and then jump off the wagon and walk up and let the wagon follow.

We were all dripping wet and it was no easy task to climb that hill through the slippery mud.

And then the scandal happened. One of the boys who had been dating a particular girl with the complete approval of her family, actually put his arm around her in public to help her up the hill. When this slipped out the whole town buzzed with her shamelessness. We all fancied there would be a speedy marriage; but that didn't happen, and the swain went further afield and the last time I was home many many years later, the girl was still a Miss. How absurd that seems to us now. But it wasn't absurd when a woman's person was sacred. One forgets how far that idea was carried. I remember well the long riding skirts that were worn by women when riding. The skirt hung about a foot below the feet of the rider, and the bottom hem was weighted down with leaden weights so that it wouldn't be possible for it to blow up and disclose a glimpse of what it was supposed to cover.

Well, we all made it to the house and started drying off. I was fitted with a pair of our host's trousers, but as he was six feet two and I five seven, it wasn't too good a fit, and I went round all evening with the trouser legs rolled up about six inches to keep them from dragging and tripping me up.

After we had dried out we had a delicious supper, which was worth the trip, and then, the storm having passed, and the moon shining again, after fresh dry hay had been put on the wagon we loaded up and drove back to town without further adventure.

I suppose at the time of all this happening I was pretty miserable, for I was extremely bashful and to be thus summarily disrobed in the presence of my whole class could have been nothing less than devastating. Now, looking back, I can remember only laughing faces, melody, and moonlight. How wonderful it is that we are blessed with a forgettery as well as a memory, and that the ability to forget cleanses our memories of all but the beautiful.

It was shortly before this time that an event occurred which was to change the whole course of American life and morals; an event which changed a nation intent only on its own growth and progress, into one looking on the whole world as its field of action.

Spain was struggling to hold the last of its western colonies; and Cuba was the scene of the outrageous blunder that Spain invariably made in dealing with other peoples. The sole purpose of Spain in holding a colony was to have something to be robbed and cheated, with never the slightest effort to provide education or social advantage of any kind. The war for Cuban liberation was accompanied by all the brutality which could possibly attend such a conflict. No one was exempt. The countryside was stripped of population, to reduce assistance to the rebels in the hills, and the people were herded into concentration camps where they underwent every deprivation, scanty food, contagious disease, squalor and filth. Much of this had appeared in the American newspapers; and the entire nation was seething with wrath that such a thing would happen at our very doors. Yet no one really wanted war. No one yet knew what was the real strength of Spain. No one felt sure that we, in a contest with what was still regarded as one of the world's great powers could come off victorious.

Then came the fatal folly of the Spanish command.

The battleship *Maine* was anchored in Havana Harbor. In the dead of night there was an explosion which sent the *Maine* to the bottom, carrying with it its crew, many of whom perished in the wreckage. The Spanish claimed that this explosion was from someone inside the ship, done with the intent of rousing the people of America and giving an excuse for a declaration of war. This hardly seems probable, as the President and his advisors were none too anxious for war. And the American people were roused enough without any provocation. It is far more probable that it was just another of the stupid acts the Spanish authorities had perpetrated in their effort to crush the Cuban people.[13]

At any rate, after that act war was inevitable.

I well remember one of the sentimental songs that all the young people were singing.

Once I had a sweetheart,
Honest, brave and true,
Fearless as the sunrise,
Gentle as the dew.
We had loved and waited,
We had named the day,
We were pledged to wed each other
In the month of May.
Cho. 1 My sweetheart went down in the *Maine,*

the rest I do not remember.[14]

This was a war which needed no draft. Camps could not be found nor arms supplied for the many who demanded enlistment.

That spirit is hard to remember. In those days we had no "Salute to the Flag,"[15] in fact we didn't regard the flag other than as a symbol of our country. It was used where use now never would be permissible, as a cover for the speaker's table at out of door rallies, picnics and the like. It was draped wherever it seemed someone wanted a touch of colour. No, we had no salutes and pledges of allegiance and the like, all we knew about the flag was to die for it.

At the Academy every boy who was of age, or who could persuade his parents to give their permission, enlisted. School attendance was cut in almost half. I was one of the ones who was too young for enlistment without my parents' consent and this they stubbornly refused to give. "Wait," they said, "if the time comes when there is a need, then go but until then stay here and prepare for living." As it turned out, it was just as well as far as any active duties were concerned. Only a very small part of the enlistees ever were called upon for active service, but most were kept in training camps under conditions almost as bad as the concentration camps in Cuba. Many died. In fact my very best school friend died in a typhoid epidemic at his camp in the south. Added to the disease, the nation was afflicted with profiteers who contracted to supply the army's needs with food, clothing etc. There was quite a scandal over packing firms supplying "embalmed" beef, some even having been found, it was claimed, to have contained formaldehyde. But almost all miserably poor and almost unfit for human food. How strange it is that even at a time like that when the whole nation was burning with patriotism and the newfound will to strike for the oppressed, there should creep out of the slime creatures in the human form whose only desire was to reap financial profit, no matter what the cost.[16]

But heroes were born and presidents created. The Rough riders with the swash-buckling Teddy at their head made their theatrical charge up San Juan Hill; and no one for a moment paid any attention to the fact that had it not been for the support of a regiment of Negro regulars, Teddy would have had to rush down as fast or faster than he charged up.[17]

As you all know, the war lasted only a very few days. Spain was found not to be a paper tiger, but not even a paper pussycat. After the battle of Manila Bay and the trapping of the Spanish fleet at Havana, and its destruction on its attempt to escape, there was nothing left for Spain but abject surrender; and America was left with the problem of what to do with the Spanish insular possessions.[18] There was bitter opposition by many of their retention; feeling that they should at once be put on their own. Many advocated the annexation of Cuba, with final statehood. Perhaps if the course had been followed, and we had used the same enlightened treatment we displayed toward the people of the Philippines we might have had in Cuba as loyal a support as we have from the eastern islands.[19] We might have had there a showcase for democracy which would have been a guiding light to all the Latin-American countries. But we proceeded neither to annex, nor to free and place on their own resources, nor fully to teach; and still retained a suzerainty which was bound to be hateful of a proud and independent people. We made our own bed with business interest which to a large extent continued the injustices of Spain. Education was neglected and wages kept at a sub standard sum and to the profit of some organizations, but to the eternal loss to the nation of the love which the Cuban was ready then to give. In fact, a love for which many years prompted him to endure more from us than we would have knowingly required.

But for the time being America emerged from the war for the first time recognized as a world power. We were as the Psalmist put it, "Rejoicing as a strong man to run a race."[20] We had whipped Spain in Jiffy order. We were prosperous at home and respected abroad. We were no longer the upstart Nation of colonists. We were America!

This was, what was to be for the next decade the Golden Age of America. Perhaps unless conditions rapidly right themselves, the decline of the American Republic will date from the end of that decade. True there were depressions during that time, and there were difficulties of many kinds; but self confident, we knew we could beat them all.

With the civil strife between Theodore Roosevelt and President Taft,[21] the era came to an end. And in a large measure, while there had been great advances made in material wealth, and in its attendant soft living, and ease of many conveniences, in the more important things of national morality both public and private, in respect for law, and in hope and ambition we grow sadly deficient.

While I am talking about the era from 1898 to 1908 there is another which I have neglected, so this will be a few words.

CHAPTER 9

Of Politics and Politicians

To understand the politics of the so called gay nineties, it will be necessary to go back several years to observe the growth and direction of public thought. When this is written in September 1967, it is just 86 years to the day since President James A. Garfield died from an assassin's bullet.[1] One can only surmise what kind of a president he would have made had he been granted more time; but his successor Chester A. Arthur proved to be a man of very mediocre ability.[2] So much was this true, and the finances of our abundantly endowed nation were in such confusion, that for the first time there was a possibility in 1884 of a Democrat being elected.[3] With unusual good judgement the leaders of that party chose Grover Cleveland of New York, and he was elected and took office in 1885.

Cleveland was in a very unenviable position. He was a man of sober ability, and in fact made one of our most outstanding presidents. But in his own day it was otherwise. He was a candidate elected by a minority party, by the dissident votes of the Republicans. And this dissidence did not endure. Soon he was the object of criticism of his policies from both parties.

There was a spirit of change in the air. Many changes were cried for which have now been accepted; but Cleveland, a sincere conservative, opposed them. The result, his defeat for a second term in 1888. His conqueror was Benjamin Harrison, a Civil War ranking officer, a good man but with little leadership ability. He was unable to change the trend toward what was then considered extreme liberalism, and as a result Cleveland did what had never before or since been done. He defeated Harrison and took over for a second term, in the election of 1892.[4]

Why these years were called the Gay Nineties is beyond me. To those of us who lived them, they were anything but gay, American manufacturers were in difficulties, and their goods were being undersold by foreign imports. The national finances were in a tangle. Farm prices were miserably inadequate, and the states of the west which had depended on their mining saw mine after mine close, with other businesses falling with them. There arose then a queer philosophy of financial affairs. Change for the better was to be made by manipulation of [the] monetary system and rate of coinage. There was a quack financier in Arkansas who called himself "Coin" Harvey who was the author of a book which became the guide of a large section of the Democratic Party. The world was to be made safe and serene by the free and unlimited coinage of silver at the ratio of sixteen silver dollars to one gold based, and by tariff for revenue only.[5]

Cleveland could see the fallacy of this idea, and had the courage to face the wrath of Colorado and other silver producing states. He alienated such a strong following in his party that the party was completely split between the "gold bugs" who were for sound money and the "Free silver men."

In the convention in 1896 the free silver men took over. A young Nebraska lawyer named William Jennings Bryan delivered his famous speech demanding that man be no longer crowned with thorns nor crucified upon a cross of gold.[6] This convention action split off the sound money democrats and many left the party never to return; and left it in a condition of hopeless minority until in 1912 the quarrel of the popular Teddy Roosevelt with his protégé and successor William Howard Taft, divided the Republican party sufficiently to permit the election of Woodrow Wilson.[7] This quarrel was a rather pitiful affair, when you could see Teddy trying to dictate to his successor, and upon his failure to do so proceeding to wreck his party and his nation rather than let the man who had stood firmly for what he himself thought was right to be elected again.

Of course, all young boys tend to declare their politics along the lines of family tradition. It is something which we inherit from our fathers, like red hair or a big nose; and as far as the usual individual is concerned, with about as little personal thought or effort. I probably was influenced to some considerable extent by this tendency, but I became an ardent supporter of McKinley, who in 1896 ended the era of Democratic control.

The elections in the nineties were ardent affairs. The list of speakers was abundant and the lure of the outdoor meeting was high. In Kansas the Populist Party was quite strong and the national Populist Party had fused with the Democrat in support of Bryan. He had no need of help along the line of crowd-pleasing oratory. In fact it was oratory that won his nomination. And I have heard him myself with breathless attention. You hung on every word, and it seemed the very epitome of logic, but when you had left the scene and the tones of the pipe organ voice no longer rang in your ears, to save your life you couldn't remember a thing he said. It always reminded me of what an old Indian from the Pottawatomie Reservation once said in a drug store. They had stiffened up the laws so strictly that he couldn't longer go in and get a snort of firewater, so he ordered a glass of strawberry soda. He sat it on the table in the booth, and it was so pretty as it bubbled away that he just sat and looked at it. When it had "blown steam" until it was only about two-thirds its original size he took a sip, then spat out with disgust "Heap big sweet wind." That was what Bryan's speeches were.

None the less had the election been held in October rather than in November Bryan would have been overwhelmingly elected. As it was enough of his party began to see to what his platform would lead, and voted for McKinley. Bryan was defeated, but he did drag into office many of the smaller candidates at state and local level. One in our own neighborhood was an unknown lawyer of little talent who was elected district judge. I believe he was more surprised than anyone else.

During the campaign that National Committee sent out good speakers wherever wanted. I have a vivid memory of one such day.

In Eureka public speeches and meetings were held on the Court House square whenever weather and the worms permitted. The Court was shaded by a fine grove of soft maple trees which gave delightful shade, but which were plagued by a variety of worm found on no other tree, which would almost denude the trees of leaves, and dropped on the unfortunate person beneath them. Then about the middle of the nineties the English sparrow found its way west, and for some reason seemed to have a special taste for these worms and in a couple of years they were things of the past. It is far different from the conduct of the present pests the Starling. I have always had a warm spot in my heart for the sturdy little brown finch without fear, bravely facing the sometimes active dislike of his fellow citizens. He has been a pest in some ways, and who doesn't have a fault or two—but he has always been a gallant ally against our insect pests. Give him credit.

Well, the platform was put up, plank seats were arranged in rows in front of it. A program was arranged giving due opportunity to be seen to local candidates and then the time fixed for the main entertainment. Of course there was the usual band to call the assembly to order.

It reminds me of a fumbling master of ceremonies to one such affair who began his introduction, "Ladies and gentlemen, the band will now play and the audience will assemble, then our friend Congressman Bumpbump will speak and then the band will again play and the crowd will again assemble."

We were in no danger of that for our speaker was to be Senator Hoar of [illegible word] with a national reputation as an orator.[8]

The senator was speaking at another town some twenty miles east of Eureka, and was to come over by buggy in time for his speech. About twenty young men and boys, well mounted, met him about a mile east of Eureka, met his equipage and escorted it in, at a quick gallop and wound up with a flourish just opposite the grand stand. I was in the height of my glory to be a member of this escort.

I don't suppose a speech such as he made would draw much interest now; but at that time when he told of the history of our nation and its achievements we were thrilled almost to tears, and when he told of the miserable management and claims of the opposition we ground our teeth in rage. When he'd hold up a piece of cutlery and shout "Look at this. Look at what it says on the blade, 'made in Sheffield England' and our own plants shut down and our workmen in want. And these Democrats not alone advocate tampering with our money, they also propose free trade, open our doors without restriction to the dumping of foreign merchandise and more cold smokestacks in factories, and more hungry Americans in bread lines! This shall not be!"

And he was right. In spite of the combination of forces against him McKinley was overwhelmingly elected. The Congress promptly passed a protective tariff which was certainly needed at the time when American manufacturers were in no condition to meet foreign condition, and the whole economy would have suffered by their failure. At the present time with the growth of great financial empires, it is the public that needs protection from the ever increasing price of merchandise and the relentless drive of some leaders of Union Labor to drive it yet higher.

After 1896 the faithful who remained loyal to the democratic faith as expressed in the 1896 platform, went so to speak under ground. They certainly did not disappear; but they did manage to secure here and there the adoption of their doctrines, until at this time almost the whole of their political philosophy has been adopted by and become the faith of the party which at present calls itself Democrat. They did make one more attempt to put it across by re-nominating Bryan, but the dew was off the rose and the bloom had left the peach and he was soundly trounced. Sound money and protection were in the ascendant and to remain there for many other campaigns.

CHAPTER 10

Opening the Indian Lands

Two other events during this era did much to stimulate the economic conditions of the states. The first was the opening of more lands to settlement and sale. The most interesting of the lands sold was probably located in what is now the State of Oklahoma. At that time, that state was divided into the Indian Territory on the east, reaching some distance west of Tulsa, Oklahoma Territory, and the Cherokee Strip, which was along the northern border of Oklahoma. The lands in the Indian Territory had been allotted to individual owners.[1] That is, the lands which had been held tribally were divided up and allotted to the members of the tribe, on the basis of their blood. Since it was generally supposed that a full blood would receive more than of mixed blood, nearly everyone tried to come under that category, with sometimes amusing results. Many were listed as full blood who had only a small amount of Indian blood. This was especially true among the Creeks where large numbers of slaves were taken into the tribe without question. This resulted in many negroes being enrolled as full blood Creeks. This was also to a quite large extent true of the Seminoles. The Indian Territory was divided into five tribal nations, the Creeks, Seminoles, Cherokees, Chickashas [Chickasaws], and Chocktaws [Choctaws]. Each tribe had its own tribal laws and customs, but was under the supervision of the Federal Commissioners and District Courts, and operating out of them, United States Marshals and Deputy Marshals. One amusing thing about this allotment system was that the Indians discovered that under the enabling act, a full blood had no right to sell his land. The result was that many listed on the full blood rolls sold their lands, time after time, for whatever anyone would offer; and when the purchaser went to take possession of the land he'd find out that his deed was no good; and in addition to that the law was so worded that he was penalized for dealing with an Indian and could in no way recover his purchase money.

One old Indian took advantage of this and sold his farm many times, and finally woke up to disaster when the Federal Congress without his knowledge removed this disability, and his last sale for a pittance was good and the buyer took over. So the biter was himself bitten.[2]

One cannot feel however, that he got what was coming to him, for the Indian had received such shabby treatment from individual whites and from the government itself, that anything he could get to offset his losses was legitimate. Here he was, dispossessed of the finest lands and the richest lands in the east, to be settled in the most picturesque, but agriculturally the most undesirable land possible. Its forests were abundant, but once they were removed, but little of value was left. It was land, most of it, in the Indian Territory part of Oklahoma, land that no one wanted. The face of fate must have radiated a thousand smiles when oil was discovered on this land, and the Indian became rich on what the white man had scorned.[3]

Looking back at the history of the white man's transactions with the Indians is not something which could rightly be said to create pride in our national honor. How many times in that history has the white man driven the native out of his home and onto lands which the white man did not want. From the fertile east, the gold mines of Georgia, the eastern valley states, and on and on, a continual evictment, and each time the treaty was made, that the new lands should belong to the Indian "as long as grass grows and water runs";[4] when it seems that grass quit growing and water running as soon as some whites found that they wanted the Indian's last reservation. How many many times that treaty was made, and how many many times it was deliberately and callously broken. And still is being broken in spirit every day, while a patriarchal Bureau of Indian Affairs keeps them with broken hearts and resentful minds, in a continued condition of semi-servitude and slavery. We will never solve our Indian difficulties until we begin to accept them as human beings and not articles of political merchandising. All our token payments of damages of late years is pitiful recompense for the suffering and deprivation of generations; and that which is still going on.

The land of the Cherokee Strip was better farming land than that east of it, well watered, and good grazing land. It too was found to be oil rich, but at this time was simply more land a great deal like the soil of Southern Kansas. When the sale of this land to settlers was finally decided it created a great deal of interest all through the neighboring areas.

It so happened that the opening was to happen about the time that my father usually got restless in the fall and decided on a camping trip. This was a fairly annual event, for the Kansas fall, like most of the mid-west, is the glory time of the year. Fall flowers are in bloom. Miles and miles of goldenrod, acres and acres of sunflowers, and the purple of elderberry and haw[5] and the sharp taste of the fox grape. And flashing from clumps along the draws, the red of the sand plum, that is puckery as a green persimmon but makes the most delicious jellies and jams I could ever get. Then too, at this time the ground cherries were ripening. Round golden balls each encased in a Chinese Lantern like pod. These little fellows, if you are not familiar with them, are really a close relative of the tomato; and were used in making one of the most delicious jams that we could find. And too, hunting would be good in the fall. The tree leaves were thinning out and it was easier to spot the elusive fox squirrel, and the bunnies would be fat and succulent.

So away we go. The four of us. Mother, Father, Bill, and I with our meager camping equipment loaded on a spring wagon. Off to some pleasant camping ground along some stream.

I remember the drive that fall, for it was not the lonely one we usually encountered. This time conveyances of every kind were streaming past us, bound for the line up at the border, or perhaps to try to slip past the guarding military and get on the land and have it staked out before the regular homesteaders entered. There were horses hitched to carriages and wagons of all sorts; some loaded with farming equipment as though the drivers expected to go immediately to work farming. There were horseback riders, and even some on foot. A few had brought special horses, animals with a reputation for speed, and had equipped them with the light English saddle and gear in place of the fifty pound stock saddle in common use.

We pitched our camp about ten miles from the starting line, where the would-be homesteaders were supposed to wait until the sound of the starting gun. Then that day there was a mad scramble; horseback riders, going at full gallop; wagons with teams galloping too, and many of them coming to grief and breaking up because they were never built for such punishment. There were fights galore, when a desirable spot was found and someone already had his stakes showing. There were claim jumpers, men of violence, who picked what they wanted and ran the prior claimant off or perhaps did a bit of actual elimination. It was a rough time and a rough crowd. But in spite of it all, the outcome was fine cities and happy farm homes.[6]

And on our way back we were again passed by the land seekers, who, disappointed in the race, were moving sadly on the way back, prepared to pick up the pieces. There were a few later land drawings in states further North, but this was the last one with the colour of former days, when might was right. The later ones were handled more methodically and were more like an ordinary business transaction.

The other event of which I spoke as momentous was the discovery of gold in the Klondike. Until this time the Alaska Purchase was regarded as either a piece of folly, paying out good money for worthless land; or else, Oh well, we'd just as well have it. Makes a good place for whalers to go, and where else would the ladies get their expensive and status creating seal skin coats?

But now, the fire of the forty-niners burned again. Men from all walks in life outfitted themselves as best as they knew how and started on another gold rush. Our small town and the Academy itself were not immune. My closest friend at this time was a son of the

Principal, Maurice Scroggs. We viewed him with somewhat of awe at his courage and rashness in braving the North. Well, he didn't suffer the fate of so many; but so far as I know the only gold he saw was in some other miner's poke, as he weighed it out in payment for merchandise at the stores.

The knowledge of the men who took part in this gold rush was so scant as to what they should have in the way of equipment, that many never reached the land of riches; leaving their bones and their hopes in some crevasse or buried under some blizzard driven snow. And most of the ones who tried, gained nothing but experience. The real money, as in all such adventures was made by the later-coming, well-equipped and financially stable companies who bought up the claims of the prospectors at a low cost, and who were prepared to do scientific mining, refining and marketing. But that is the way such things generally go. The local citizen himself seldom profits from such a discovery. Perhaps partially due to his sustained feeling that the ground is worthless or that the find is greatly exaggerated, so makes no effort to profit from it himself.[7]

CHAPTER II

Social Life in a Small Town

One thing I must not forget to record, and that is a glimpse of the social life in a small town. For regulated and planned social living is as old as the hills themselves. All peoples have had and will continue to have their taboos; their conservatives; their "way outs"; nothing new under the sun; just expressed in different ways.

Of course the social life of that day both in the cities and in the rural towns was largely centered about the church. The affairs of the church societies were special events; and the churches gave the women of that day an opportunity for community service they now, in their more distracting circumstances seem to have lost. And perhaps it is a greater loss than we will admit; for the life of a nation is inescapably based on and a reflection of its religion. No matter what the faith may be, no nation can long survive without one of some sort. Men must have something by which they can put the seal of verity upon their neighbor's oath. And 'tis sadly true that as the citizen's religious convictions decline the nation declines. Perhaps it may endure for a time but its end is as inevitable as that of a girdled tree.[1]

One of the principal things that has disappeared was the "day at home." Every lady had announced and set apart for her day to be at home and receive. Other days she might excusably be away when a friend called, but that day, well known in her set, she dare not. The guests came, and sometimes stopped for a short visit and perhaps a bit of refreshment, others just stopped and left their cards. Oh yes, every woman carried her card case, and as beautifully printed or engraved a card as was available. I well remember my mother's card case of mother of pearl. It was always ready and always with its stock of cards. Since my mother was unable to walk to these affairs, it was my duty to put old Don to the phaeton and be her transportation. In case you don't know what a phaeton is, or rather was, it was a single seated rig, hung very low to the ground, with no sides to the body to be stepped over, and a folding top. It was usually larger or wider than the common buggy and was a very popular ladies rig, as it was easy to enter, and there was adequate width so a wheel could be "cramped," that is turned out to give wider entering space between the front and back wheel. The back wheels were covered by leather fenders to protect the ladies' skirts from dust or mud.

The quilting bee was another social affair, usually confined to one's home or to meetings of the ladies' church societies. Some there were who had a special skill in the dainty needlework required and they were always specially welcomed. But most women could "sew a fine seam" and one that was good enough. The pieces and scraps of cloth sometimes had special memories attached. I have seen whole quilts made from neckties that had been discarded, and some from specially saved bits of dresses. Most women kept a "rag bag" and in it accumulated swatches of cloth that they thought would be desirable. This cloth was cut into [?][2] about an inch and a half square, and these squares were sewn together in the desired pattern until the whole was large enough to cover a bed. Then a sheet of plain white was fastened to a set of quilting frames, narrow strips of wood large enough to hold the whole quilt in place and stretched taut. The bottom was covered with a layer of cotton, and the quilt top placed above it. Then the quilting was done by sewing through top, cotton and bottom with very fine stitches, done in some well-known design. I can't remember them all, but there was "Herring bone" and "Sunrise" and many many others and most women adept at them all. The pattern was sometimes lightly marked on the top in pencil to be followed by the seamstresses, but there were some so expert that they needed no design. After a strip along the frame had been sewed until it was hard to reach farther in, the frame was loosened and the finished part rolled up, the frame was again fastened and another strip stitched, and so on until the whole was quilted. Then the quilt was removed from the frame and binding sewn around the raw edges, and you had a truly attractive bit of bedding. These quilts were sometimes made and saved to make for the daughter of the house an adequate supply for her after marriage. Some were sold at church bazaars, and the money used largely in helping finance the mission work of the church. These quilting bees were truly happy occasions. When you get fifteen or twenty ladies seated about the quilting frame, which was balanced on the backs of chairs, and when the needles were flashing and conversation bubbling, everyone really had an enjoyable afternoon, which they left with a feeling of having not only spent a pleasant time, but of having done something worthwhile for the good of the community.

I spoke before of the Medicine Shows, but we had a real theatre all of our own. There were traveling about the country innumerable groups of repertory players who visited the local "Oprey houses" all winter long. There were few months that didn't have one or two of these weeklong performances. This was generally called the "Kerosene Circuit" due to the fact that the stage lights were coal oil lamps placed around the front of the stage and with their brightness directed toward the stage and away from the audience by a bright, unpainted tin shield.[3] I always loved these shows, for they often did a very good job on such plays as Quo Vadis, East Lynn, sometimes a Shakespearean, sometimes pure slapstick comedy.[4] Many of the players on the Kerosene graduated to the "Gas Light Circuit" in the cities and became famous names of the stage. I always liked to attend these shows, and as money was not plentiful enough or to spare, I wangled a job as an usher. Then after the audience had been seated I'd have my chair reserved at the side of the stage where I could enjoy the rest of the evening.

These "Oprey Houses" were really vacant loft rooms over a couple of adjoining stores, which had been thrown together and a stage erected at one end with dressing rooms at each side, and seating provided by rows of ordinary kitchen chairs fastened together by a board running under the seat of eight or ten chairs and nailed firmly fast. Not much to look at, but the epitome of sophistication and pleasure to me. And really the world has suffered a great loss when these troupes vanished. No TV can ever replace them.

There were Sunday School picnics; all day long. We had one particular grove which we always used. There the natural trees had not been cut or marred. The great oaks and walnuts stood with huge arms outspread, offering themselves to us to hold the swings. Since I was light of weight and strong, there would be a rope thrown over a great limb high above and held in place while I went up it hand over hand and perched on the limb to make the final double knots. There were tables heaped with food. Real food! There were gallons on gallons of homemade ice cream, yellow as butter and delicious as ambrosia.

Close to this picnic ground, Fall River slipped gently, about a foot in depth for several hundred yards, over solid rock bottom smooth as a floor, making a perfectly safe place for the smaller children to play in safety, while farther on, just around a bend was the "round hole," wide and deep where the larger boys and men could take their pleasure. I got myself nearly drowned there one day when I, by no means an expert swimmer, dove in, forgetting to remove those blasted "specs" and came up unable to see where I wanted to go and panicked and gulped in about ten gallons of Fall River water before I could be dragged out.

The young people had mixed parties.[5] At them, they danced the old folk dances, the Virginia Reel,[6] and the like. And post office was a game they all, under adequate supervision, were allowed to play. There the boys sat in one room and the girls in another and the master of ceremonies would call out the name of a boy, that there was for him, a postcard, or a special delivery, or a letter, or a registered letter, each one signifying some particular mark of affection. He'd go into another room and there find a little lady ready to make a delivery. I can remember the few times when someone sent me a registered letter, how I'd go in, trembling and embarrassed, accept the quick and timid touch of warm lips and then go back to the boys' room amid laughter and blushes. Where are those warm lips now? I often tell my children about how bashful I was as a boy, only to be caught with "Wow! How times have changed!"

I have been talking so much about the children and the ladies that I have completely ignored the men.

Well, of course they took part in church affairs too; but their main meetings were at political rallies and at the secret societies of which there were many. The Masonic Order and Eastern Star are still going strong, but many of their rivals have dropped by the wayside or dwindled to negligible numbers. There were the Odd Fellows, The Workmen, The Knights and Ladies of Security, The Knights of Pythias, and many more.[7] Most of them operated a life insurance department based on impossible rate which, as the members advanced in age and were no longer the young and vigorous men who organized the order, had to be raided again and again until the cost became prohibitive and many of the members were left without insurance and only able to obtain more by paying high rates to some old line company which was actuarially sound.

Of course there was always door to door visiting. We had neighbors next door, not just people we didn't know and didn't want to know. This neighborliness still exists a bit in smaller towns, but even there is vanishing as more and more distractions make such social living too difficult, and there again we have lost, more than we could possibly gain.

Then too, nearly every family had its own particular pass times. With me, it was taking the phaeton and driving aimlessly about the country with my mother as passenger. Driving out into the fields in spring when the pastures were carpeted with white or purple anemonae, so thick that it was a solid blanket which billowed and swayed in the spring wind. That was my special name for these pretty blooms, wind flower.[8]

But each season had its special beauties. One of our ways of spending an evening, when the big, soft summer clouds dotted the evening blue, was to hunt and point to each other the changing pictures they made. Oh, look there, (pointing) see that horse and rider? No, now it's changing to a man's face. See, there's a blue lake with snow-clad shores, and a white boat moored to the edge. And so on, and on. If I have been blessed with a happy imagination, it has been due to the insight of my school teacher mother, who never tired in leading me on to see, to hear and to understand.

The year 1899 was in many ways a disappointment, yet in many ways a good year in my life. I had hoped to enter college after my graduation from the academy in 1898; but financial difficulties rendered this impossible. My older brother had intended to go to the State University, but after he had remained out of school one year he lost all desire to do other than work at his chosen trade, of an electrician. That was something new for small towns. The only street lights we had had were the lanterns we carried in our own hands. But progress was moving our way and Bill went to the State University in the Electrical Engineering department and managed to fit himself with a working knowledge sufficient to enable him to return to Eureka and put in its first electrical light system. The street lights were an arc light swinging above each street intersection in the most traveled streets. These arc lights gave a brilliant illumination but had the greatest nuisance value of any light ever devised by man. Behind a huge globe, two sticks of carbon, about the size of a man's finger were held in place with their ends just meeting. They were then wired into an electric circuit which heated the terminals white hot as the current poured across the gap. But they had to be lowered each morning and out of the globe take the accumulation of bugs, great and small, that had committed suicide during the night, trim and reset the carbons and make ready for the next evening. There was usually about a quart of bugs in each globe. One of the funniest mishaps I have ever seen happened under such a light at an out of doors concert, where the singer in an extremely low bodiced gown, had one of the larger night beetles miss the globe and come tumbling down inside her dress. The song stopped and the singer's antics in trying to displace her unwelcome visitor were the best act of the show.

Mother was determined I should not do the same as brother Bill; so back to S.K.A.[9] I went for a final year, reviewing and perfecting the courses I had previously studied. That way I was to keep the feel of being in school; and it was far from a bad idea. I really think I got more solid understanding of my previous studies than I would have had any other way.

In another way this was a special sort of year, 1899, the final year of a century. Now don't start the old dispute whether the year 1900 was the last year of the 19th century or the first year of the 20th. I don't know and I doubt if anyone else could give an unanswerable verdict. But we all treated 1899 as the final year of the century.

That was the beginning of an era I have formerly mentioned, which could be well classed as the golden age of America. And it was to bring to me an entirely new environment and new sets of ideas. It was well that we celebrated the New Year. And all over the nation from one shore to the other "Fin de siecle"[10] parties were organized. I doubt, even in this day of uproarious and blatant exhibitionism that ever a more noisy and jubilant New Year's day could be celebrated.

My particular group of friends decided to hold our Watch Party at the home of two classmates at the edge of town.

This home was one of the show places. A large and for the day luxurious home stood in the midst of a grove of beautiful pine, near to natural wood land. The grounds were always beautifully kept, and about them strolled gaudy, and absurdly proud pea fowl. These birds were more than mere ornament. No one living in the immediate neighborhood needed an early morning mill whistle to awaken them. It was the habit of the male birds to soar gracefully to the roof of the house and there meet the dawn with outspread tail as multicolored as the dawn itself, and announce the new day by the most gosh awful scream ever heard by mortal man. Fortunately it didn't last more than a minute or two.

There we were gathered, and most of the evening which was not devoted to games or music was spent in talk of our future. We all knew that this was probably the last gathering of a group that had been playmates and fellow students from the early grades. And now that would in a few months be all past us, and we would separate into what other unknown places and lives none could guess. While we looked forward to it with anticipation, there was a bit of fear in it too.

The songs we sang were old songs. Like so many of that day they were rather sad and nostalgic. But we had grown up on the songs of the civil war days, and that was all the sort we knew. They did tell us that in the cities a new sort of music that was called Rag Time was taking hold but it hadn't penetrated yet the hinterland.

Then, just as the clock passed the midnight mark, for some unknown reason Mr. Pea Cock who should have been sound asleep, opened from the roof with that yell which would have made the rebel yell at Gettysburg seem faint. Don't know what caused it. Perhaps he had some orders from some great authority to announce the change.

It was as natural that I should enter Washburn College as for me to breathe. All S.K.A. men went to Washburn. Reason, it was a school founded and supported by the Congregational Church as was the academy. And all Washburn graduates who wanted to go on for a higher degree went just as naturally to Yale. Washburn founded in 1865 was just 35 years old when I entered, and a few years ago I celebrated with a few surviving older graduates its century mark.[11]

Since finances hadn't improved too much, father decided that the only way to send me to school was to take me to school. That is to actually move to the school town where I then could board at home and perhaps help out with my own efforts in a place of greater opportunity for self-help.

To accomplish this, father sold his business and our home in Eureka and took over a small business in Topeka, handling musical instruments, sewing machines, and various other items. This business had been rather a poor prospect for survival, but with father's energy and perseverance it was the foundation of a business which supported him until his final retirement, due to advancing age.

I hope to tell you more about the college days at the beginning of the century; vastly different from today, but that is the story for another day. Now we will turn the page and say goodbye to the two small towns of my boyhood and youth; places that I now remember with increasing appreciation.

CHAPTER 12

Life in Topeka

Thanks to my frequent stays in Kansas City, the change of home grounds wasn't as much of a revelation.

Topeka, in the year 1900 was a clean, attractive little city, with a population of around thirty-five thousand and claiming fifty.[1] It had been planned by men of vision, and as a result the streets were unusually wide. Kansas Avenue, the main business street being about twice the breadth of city streets. All principal streets were paved with what, for the day, was up to date material, having been covered with a layer of sand, on which heavy planks were laid and the whole covered with heavy paving brick standing on edge and helped in staying firm by a layer of sand on top which was swept into the few crevasses between the bricks. This made a very solid pavement, but one inclined in time, as the under foundation settled or gave way, to assume rather a roller coaster profile, and to be noisy in the extreme. Add to this that there were many vehicles equipped only with iron tires, and that didn't help matters. In 1900 there was just one automobile in Topeka. That was a single seated Oldsmobile, with an umbrella for shade. I can't remember the name of the owner, but he kept the car garaged in a building on the alley running North and

Bolinger family on the porch of the family home at 935 Morris Avenue, Topeka, Kansas, circa 1900. *From left to right:* Della Bolinger, William A. Bolinger (A. J.'s brother), Delia Bolinger (Ada Delia Hostetter Bolinger, A. J.'s mother), William H. Bolinger (A. J.'s father), William M. Bolinger, Julia (?), and Babetta (?). Identification from notations on back on photograph. (Photograph courtesy of Bruce Bolinger)

South, half a block west of Eighth and Kansas. But the time of the auto was at hand and by the year 1906 there [were] many automobiles; and Smith Brothers had transformed their truss factory into a car manufactory, featuring the Great Smith.[2] As a matter of fact at that era there were few towns of any size that didn't have one or more car factories.

My first car was a Great Smith, and a hint as to its primitive nature can be guessed by the fact that once when I ran off the road into a ditch the strain broke the two 4 × 4 wooden beams that were the frame, so that the front wheels and engine ran to the right and the body and the hind wheels came to a sudden stop. Far from ruining the car, the garage operator simply got two more four by fours and went out and removed the two that were broken and bolted in the two new ones and we were off, good as ever.

It might be of interest for me to describe some of these early vehicles. Among the first was the Oldsmobile, the production of a manufacturer R. E. Olds; who later was bilked out of his company and formed a new company to produce the REO.[3] Buick too was an early entrant with a two-seated car with a buggy top cover, a two cylinder engine under the front seat. Of course no car at that time had either front or rear doors, and the windshield hadn't appeared; and of course there were no self-starters. They didn't come into general use until nearly fifteen years later, and even then the cautious motorist always carried a crank so that if the battery or starter failed he could crank up and go on any way. One of the strangest looking was the Brush, a single seated affair with a huge one-cylinder engine perched on a platform ahead of the small body. As I remember it this single cylinder was about eight inches in diameter. This particular machine was a great favorite with the doctors, making the house to house calls. I can remember them so well, the little "bug" as we called them chugging down the street trailing a cloud of black smoke. Mufflers were as yet not in common use. Then there was the Stafford, once made in Topeka and later moved to Kansas City. This was, for the time an excellent model. There was only one closed car in use and that was an electric, which was much in use by the ladies. It was a black affair, somewhat like the front half of a hearse had plate glass doors and windows, seated two, was steered by a tiller, a single lever, in place of a wheel and even had a cut glass container for flowers next to the front window. Closed gasoline cars did not come into general use until around 1918. They were regarded as top heavy and dangerous. And even as late as 1924, many still used the open "Touring car." The Stutz Bear Cat, the Maxwell, and on and on; they are all gone. Even the stately Packard has left the roads; and the humble Ford now flaunts in royal robes.[4]

There was the Stutz Bear Cat, which was the hot rod car of the day; the old Stanley Steamer and the White Steamer[5] which both had steam pressure engines and which were very popular in the mountains because they would not stall; the valveless Elmore, which as the name would indicate was equipped with rotary admittance gates to the cylinders which eliminated the bogy of fouled up spark plugs.[6]

The gasoline was of such a low rating that engines would load with carbon, and the standard way was to take off the top and shoot gas down each cylinder and burn out the deposits in a shower of blazing sparks. Without this the cylinders would lose power and develop a shaking knock and the car would have little speed or power. When you stopped at a gasoline pump the gas was not put directly into your car, but into a gasoline can first. It was pumped into the can a gallon at a time by hand pump and was always put in through a chamois skin lining the funnel into the can. When you got a five gallon can filled there was frequently strained out and lying on the chamois as much as a cup or more of water, for the chamois while it let gas through would not let the water. There was the Maxwell, the Reo, the Sears Roebuck if you please,[7] which was just an old fashioned buggy with an engine in it connected by a large leather belt to an inner grooved wheel almost as large as the back buggy wheel to the inside of which it was attached. This car was a great favorite in the rural areas because it was handier in negotiating the rough and unpaved country lanes. There were frequent car races to some fixed point by proud car owners. I well remember one about 1914 in which three cars participated. They were to go to a farm home about ten miles from town, turn round, and come back. One car only made it half way and broke down completely, the second car got to the farm house and had to be hauled by team from there back to home base, and the third which did make the trip took from noon well past sundown to get back, with its acetylene lamps barely showing the way. So on and on with hundreds of these old time cars, now long gone. But I digress:

We moved to Topeka in July, 1900, coming in what was called an Emigrant Car. This plan of shipment was one devised by the railroads to help induce farmers to come west and buy railroad lands. All through the west the government had subsidized railroads by giving them a certain number of sections of land, or a tract of land along their right of way. These lands could be sold to settlers and the money of course used in financing the railways. If they could show a farmer in the east where good lands could be obtained at low prices and how he could get there without too much expense he was far more apt to become a purchaser.[8]

In these Emigrant cars, for one low price, the emigrant, or anyone for that matter, could move his household goods, his farming equipment, livestock, and himself and family.

So in our Emigrant car for the ride which would consume some 18 hours attached to a slow freight train, mother and the other members of the family intending to come next day by passenger, was my old friend, my buggy horse Don, my horse. All our household goods were at the other end, and all and sundry other possessions filled most of the car's remaining space, leaving a space about the width of a freight door where father and I camped down for the night. We had one surprise. Knowing that we were apt to get hungry before we were anywhere where food was available, father had had the local restauranteur prepare a basket lunch, based on three chickens father himself had supplied. We left Eureka about noon, and at suppertime when we went to eat were surprised that the chickens had turned into wings of various sizes.

Father had rented a home and in a few days we were moved in and settled, and I had found my way to the college campus to view the scenes of my future efforts.

Washburn College, under the name of Lincoln College was actually begun in 1865. There had been previous competition between Topeka and Lawrence; and Topeka first had the offer of the college and was committed to take it, but fell down on their commitment, and the college was then offered to and accepted by Lawrence, but again Lawrence too failed to make good its financial backing and the offer was again revolved to Topeka. Hard times continued to plague the school, and its life was doubtful until in 1868 Deacon Ichabod Washburn of Worcester, Massachusetts, being advised of the character of the school and its purpose, made what was for then a very large gift, the sum of $25,000.00. Knowing that Lincoln College well could have failed save for this generous gift the Trustees changed the name of the school to Washburn College.[9]

This donor was himself a remarkable man. With little formal education and having to quit such schooling as was possible at the age of nine, he worked long hours in for a trunk and Harness Maker and then in 1812 returned to his coastal home to work in a textile mill and stand watch on the coast at night for hostile ships. Later

Arthur Joel Bolinger, Washburn College graduation picture (?), no date. (Photograph courtesy of Mary Margaret Concannon)

he was apprenticed to a blacksmith and after he became a journeyman, his feel for metal led him to experiment in wire making, an industry which the European manufacturers had held a monopoly by their carefully guarded secrets of the process. Starting with almost no knowledge, he taught himself, invented his own tools and dies;

and soon was producing as good a quality of merchandise as the imported. He regarded as his greatest achievement when he made for Chickering the first acceptable American made piano wire. Perhaps because of his own scanty schooling, and his realization of what that meant, he became deeply interested in education and became its friend and patron.

And Washburn in 1900 was the school that would have delighted Washburn's deeply religious nature. For it was definitely a church school. There were no Fraternities or Sororities; in fact the faculty and student body didn't have time for anything of the sort, and did not desire them, as they felt that they were only the result of snobbery; and that the little good they did to the accepted member was poor recompense for the heart ache of the rejected.

Young Men's Christian Association and Young Ladies Christian Ass'n., were strong; and held weekly meetings at the room of one of the students a group leader having been selected who was supposed to prepare and conduct discussion on some religious topic. There were also Temperance Clubs of both sexes and no quicker way could a student acquire the bad graces of his fellows than by appearing not only in an intoxicated condition, but even with the odor of liquor on his breath or person.

Chapel was held every morning. This room which served also as the place for college theatricals, and public meetings in general, was a large auditorium on the second floor [of] the fine cut stone building nearest the campus entrance. Alas, that building is no more, having been completely demolished in the terrible cyclone of 1966. So much of our school time was centered about this building, that without it no matter what the restoration, things, to an old grad, will never be the same.

In chapel the boys sat in class groups on one side of the central aisle, the girls in the same manner on the other. Each class had its monitor to take roll, and the student who did not answer to his name at Chapel was marked absent for the day and no matter what happened in class he simply wasn't at Washburn. The faculty had to attend also; being seated in front of the students on the large stage at the front of the auditorium. There were songs, religious in nature, a professor would read the morning lesson and give a short talk, and then the audience sedately pass down the stairs, in column of twos, and on to the next classroom. Sometimes we got a surprise in the teacher's talks too. Now and then one would make a slip which would be cherished and discussed for some time thereafter. But the greatest surprise was one day we were told that the talk would be by the German professor, a rather dour man, who was not disliked but not greatly liked either and we all anticipated a boring session. To our surprised delight, this man, with an utterly dead pan face, gave us the funniest, the most hilarious little gem that ever was heard in that hall. It may have seemed uproariously funny because it was unexpected; but this I know, this man became about the most popular professor on the campus. And he responded in his own sober way once the ice was broken.

At this time there were only three buildings in active use for class sessions, they were the basement of the McVicar Chapel, the various floors of Rice which had been the first building erected when Washburn was a one building school, and the basement of Boswell. The classrooms were all heated by a large coal-burning stove in each room, with a big coal box close at hand to keep the fires burning during the day. This coal box came in for one rather unusual use. One of our Professors, a fiery little dark-skinned Highland Scot, with the incongruous name of Harshberger, or "Harsh" as we all called him, loved his chewing tobacco and we all would secretly smile as we would see him with a bulge in his cheek growing larger, furtively directing our attention to some mathematics problem on the black board, while he slipped to the coal box and got rid of the excess moisture. What would you think of that nowadays. But this man, who was the head and all the staff of the Mathematics Department was loved by every student under him. It was his complete unassuming humanness. One tale he told me of himself will show his traits better than a long description. Harsh was always a lover of flowers and of gardening, and at the rate of pay prevalent in Washburn a good vegetable garden could come in might handy to a professor; and his was always tops. He told me of his continual trouble of chasing a neighbor's chickens out of the garden beds, and how he finally lost his temper and killed one and started to the neighbor's home with the dead biddy, when almost to the dividing line he met the neighbor lady, bringing him a fresh cake she had just baked. "And there I stood," he said, "Looking like a fool and feeling more than that; and all I could do was apologize and exchange the dead biddy for the cake." It didn't seem to have affected the affection of the lady for him, but I can't say whether she baked any more cakes, or whether the chickens kept on pestering.[10]

All during my college days, one fixture on the campus was Tom. This was a colored man who kept the huge campus in beautiful trim. He and his big team of mules could be seen, day in and day out mowing the grass, hauling away dead branches, cutting hay on the south part of the campus, working in and around the classrooms, and plowing paths through the snow. And Tom knew the name of every boy and girl on campus, usually around 400. And they were all of them his friends. It's hard to find such faithful friends and allies any more. Tom wasn't a servant, he was a member of a team and far from the least important member. God rest him.

One other teacher I must mention; for she did much for me. That was the English teacher Charlotte Mendell Leavitt. It was in her classroom that I had a loose knowledge of literature bound together and made whole. And many of the books she brought to my attention are still old friends upon my shelves, their covers broken and their leaves torn by reading and re-reading. For it was her idea and one I have found to be most accurate that no book was worth reading once unless it was worth reading more than once.[11]

Washburn campus was about a mile from downtown Topeka and could be reached by a trolley line. The Topeka system in this connection was one all its own. At 8th and Kansas Avenue stood a "Transfer Station." A passenger desiring to transfer from one line to another had to ride down to this transfer station and wait there in the shelter until a car going his way happened along. In this manner I, who lived North of Washburn, had to take a Lowman Hill car and ride a mile East to the Transfer station, and there change to another car and ride a mile southwest to school. Naturally this system wasn't much used unless in inclement weather. It was quicker and easier to walk.

Washburn students worked almost to a man. My own particular task was carrying newspapers. These we bought from the printer at 8 cents each per week and sold for 10 cents. I carried about 300 papers, at first drove a little open wagon with an old horse who knew the route so well I didn't need to touch a line or guide in any way except to keep her from turning in toward a place where the customer had moved or quit. And once she had gone past, the next evening she would pass up the place of herself. Later I carried the route horseback, and was doing so the time when the 1903 flood covered all of North Topeka where my route lay. The last night I had carried before the flood I had gone to the North end of the route, finished my deliveries and turned back and had only ridden a little way when I approached a low bit of street and before I realized it my pony was swimming; so quickly had the waters risen. But I made it out without further incident and just in time.

The next day all of North Topeka was flooded, and many of its people trapped, had to be brought out in boats. They were transported by boat to the north end of the Kansas Avenue bridge, which arched above the Kaw River, walked to the south end, and crossed another strip of about 100 yards of flood water in a breeches buoy[12] which a number working on and around a floating walk, anchored out of the current had managed to construct.

I have spoken about the deeply religious atmosphere at Washburn. One factor in keeping this condition was the pastor of Central Congregational Church which most of the faculty and students attended. This was Dr. Charles M. Sheldon, author of *In His Steps*. He was a constant inspiration and was a close friend to most of the students. To show this man's character, I can do no better than to tell of one of his exploits. The editor of the *Topeka Daily Capital*, the morning daily invited him to publish the paper one week in the form he believed Christ would use. This coming event was widely publicized, and everyone was waiting to see what kind of a paper they would get. To their surprise, the paper was a newspaper and not a religious tract. But it was a newspaper filled with current events, with emphasis on the constructive things and no play for sensationalism; and one thing notably missing was the customary liquor and tobacco ads. He remarked to those who asked him why this was his idea of the Christian paper, he answered that he was publishing a newspaper and not preaching a sermon. Another bent of his was what he called Christian Socialism. That every man must be given an opportunity;

and he who had share to create that opportunity. A lot of us were so impressed by this idea that we started a Socialist Club, of which I was elected president, and got nearly kicked out of college for my pains. Washburn was staunchly Republican and Conservative.[13]

In 1901, at Washburn, as everywhere else in the Sunflower State, the public event of greatest importance was the crusade of Carrie Nation. This pugnacious little lady from Wichita, tiring of the ineffectiveness of the enforcement of the Kansas Prohibition Laws, took upon herself a one-man war on all illegal operations.[14]

Things in Kansas had changed during the three decades since the adoption of the [Kansas] Prohibition Amendment. A system had been worked out by the thirsty, whereby a dealer did not have to pay a license, but once a month was arrested and went to police court and paid a fixed penalty for the right to be undisturbed for another month. This so-called "Fine system" was in full operation over the state; with the only requirement that the saloon, or "blind pig" had to keep its doors and windows screened from outside observation, and do no advertising. This was hardly necessary once the location of an oasis became a matter of common knowledge. However I did know one feisty little Irish operator who had the words "Fine wines and liquors" painted boldly on the front awning. However the printing was in Gaelic and who in Kansas outside a visiting Irishman could read that.

Well, the fever in Topeka rose high as elsewhere in the state. And Washburn with its close religious affiliation was stirred. Carrie was coming and to make ready for her a regiment of crusaders was formed. As I now recollect it there were some twelve hundred members in the active group, who had the support of about the entire community.

This group was organized on a strict military formation. Dr. McFarland, pastor of the First Methodist Church, was the colonel. I don't remember now who the other officers were, but we had a company at Washburn as a matter of course. And as much of a matter of course the writer was in the thick of it. We met and drilled in secret, with guards out a la KKK and some of the troopers were even encouraged to purchase and carry firearms.

The fever was at its highest stage when Carrie arrived.

Rally to be at the First Methodist, in the large stone church still standing at Sixth and Harrison. Of course the crusaders were out in force; and after the first main rally, Carrie asked some of us college boys to remain for a moment's discussion. The proposal she made to us was that she knew all the Topeka Saloons would be bolted and barricaded and she wanted some way to get into them rapidly, at night, one after another. Sixteen of us from Washburn volunteered. To the life of me I can't remember the names of any of the other participants. We had been studying ancient history and the wars and sieges of forts and castles, and we put our studying for once to a practical use. We procured from the lumberyard a four by four beam. I can't remember the exact length, but it was long enough that after we had bored holes through it and pushed through sections of iron pipe left sticking about two feet [on] either side, we could pick it up, eight to the side and swing it back and forth with comfort.

We met before the first break of dawn at the transfer station at Eighth and Kansas.

I can't remember how many saloons we worked at but I do remember two in particular. One was the Palms located about the middle of the eight hundred block on Kansas, this the most fashionable one in town. It was equipped with all the elegance of a first class city saloon, the only difference that the front show windows were curtained off and contained only a large potted palm in each window. This place was the meeting place of Kansas politicians, especially members of the legislature, refreshing themselves after a hard day's work inventing new laws to curb the demon drink. But it had its share of the local elite as well. What made it such a political headquarters was its nearness to the Copeland Hotel, at Ninth and Quincy. This hotel was known as Copeland County, and was Republican political headquarters at all times, as well as the residence of the Hon. John C. Pollock, the one Federal District Judge in Kansas at that time. He was reputed to be a man of great sharpness in his speech, and severity on any lawyer who dared make a mistake in his Court. Perhaps he was. But I had been his paperboy, and to me after I commenced my law practice he was always a kind and understanding mentor.

The other saloon whose name I can't recollect was on east 8th Street just back of the Topeka State Journal Building.

We approached the Palms first with Carrie Nation in the lead. When we were at the door she stepped aside and said "Open her up boys" and sixteen strong young sets of arms swung the battering ram against the lock. No iron or wood could stand against such blows and at the second stroke the door flew wide. Carrie stepped quickly inside, and back of the mahogany bar, and quick swings of her trusty hatchet, sent bottles and glasses flying, ripped down the voluptuous lady reclining in scanty garments that hung above the back bar, while others turned over tables and smashed chairs until all left the place a complete shambles, reeking to heavens with the odor of sanctity and spilled bourbon and rye, with the beer taps still frothing at the mouth.

We performed the same gracious act at the bar on east Eighth Street and of how many more I can't remember. The sentiment of the community was so strong that none of us young miscreants ever got out of it more than a halo. Carrie was arrested several times, and was her own defense counsel, but I can't remember of her ever suffering any severe punishment. Her trials, I remember, were before Hon. Zachary Taylor Hazen, Judge of the Shawnee County, District Court whom Carrie insisted on addressing as "Your Dishonor" rather than your Honor. She felt that this was his better title, engaged as he was in persecution of the saints.

Not alone was Carrie "agin likker"; she was also against the stinking weed and woe to the man who stepped into an elevator on which she was a passenger, holding a cigar in his teeth or hand. He had it immediately snatched and trampled under her feet, and then receiving a lecture for the rest of the passage.

Carrie was rather small, and thick set, with a snub nose and burning eyes. And her crusade was not for profit, had it been she could have made millions. She was devoted to her call, and this one woman so stirred the great Sunflower State that it was but a short time until the legislature passed the "Bone Dry" law. This law made it not only a crime to sell alcoholic liquor, but also to possess it, no matter how or where purchased, unless the bottle bore the prescription of a regularly licensed physician. The old easy days had gone, and it was no longer possible to step into a drug store and buy a bottle of medicinal liquor for any disease you might choose, sign a register and go out in perfect responsibility, or the easier way patronize a speak-easy. The rigid enforcement of the Bone Dry law was one of the main factors in securing the final repeal of the prohibition amendment.[15]

We have written much already concerning the college life, but there are many more things which might well be told, and some that must be told if you are to get a correct idea of what this fresh water College really was.

Scholastically its standing has always been high. But in the early days of this century it was even more so than it is now. The student was required to take courses in the humanities that now would seem unreasonable. But that more exacting curriculum was inherent in all schools of the time. By the time I had left the academy at Eureka I had already had four years of Latin, and one additional review year; two years of French, and one year of German which I took to sharpen up my grammar as I had already learned to speak some German at home; and math through calculus, and other studies in about that extent. At Washburn my requirements for A.B. were four years more of Latin, four years of Greek, four years of higher math, plus psychology, sociology, Logic, and English. I was able to elect two courses a year and put them in with French and German again, with side courses in oratory etc. If you will add up the hours of solid subject required for an A.B. degree in 1900 you will find them equal or above the requirements for an M.A. at the present time.

I know that the modern idea is to cut everything that is not materially useful in a business or professional career; but in their attempts to do this, education has suffered. College in place of being the means of broadening minds and developing character has become a mere status symbol.

But even with those long hours of heavy lessons, plus the time that must be used in earning the money to stay in college, the student's life was far from dull.

In the earlier days, and in fact until this century the main competitive efforts were forensic. Washburn had always relied heavily on rhetoric and oratory, and most of the other colleges did the same. There were intercollegiate debates, and oratorical contests and the like. Washburn's principal rivals were Kansas University at Lawrence and Baker University at Baldwin. Baker was a Methodist-oriented school, and the rival religious attachment, sad to say, added to the zest of the competition. There were two literary societies in my time, the Washburn College Literary Society and the Gamma Sigma. These groups met once a week for practice of their oratorical skills, and at frequent intervals for contests between the two clubs. But their rivalry was not only oratorical, it extended to the entire student life. The two clubs comprised the two political parties of the campus. W.C.L.S. being the older of the twain always tried to lord it over the humble Gamma Sigs, of which I was a member, but we finally put them in their place and for some time controlled the officers and other functions of the student body. Does this seem childish? Well, as a matter of fact it was wonderful training for future participation in politics. These two societies lingered for many years, even after athletics had claimed the brighter place in the spotlight.

Football was just beginning, in the late nineties, to be a popular sport. No rules had been adopted, no limit on players, save that they must be enrolled in some college course; and no group or league in existence. You played with whatever team you could get against anyone who would accept your challenge.

My first year, 1900–01 was the banner year for Washburn. The team that Harshberger had coached, came into full flower. Harsh had managed to instill in them some of his fire and had accumulated a line of players that were to prove invincible. At that time, football was a game of brute force. The pass was not used to any extent. When the teams lined up, face to face they hit each other like a pair of steam rollers; piled up in tangled heaps of legs and arms and often came out sadly the worse for wear. That was the year that the line up contained a welder from the Santa Fe boiler works who was enrolled in a class in religion, and the driver of the hook and ladder truck of the Topeka Fire Department who was enrolled in music. Just how much they did in their respective classes I wouldn't say. The team also had Bob and Jimmie Stewart, Jimmie the star quarterback. Then there was Frank Leach and "Fanny" Mehl, the others I can't now recall, but I knew every face that appeared in a recent number of the Washburn alumnus. That year Washburn took every competitor, including our bitter rival KU. And that was the year we earned the lasting spleen of the university by making a parody of their college yell of

rock chalk, jay hawk, k. u.
as shouted lustily by our cheerers,
squawk squawk hen hawn hoo doo.

Basketball was a girl's game. They played it among women students, but no one thought much of it.

[The manuscript is missing a page at this point.]

[The manuscript resumes in the middle of a sentence.]

. . . rumored that one student had carried and angrily displayed a revolver. So that the 1900 effort became the last of the historic cane rushes. The faculty firmly and immovably said no more such conduct by young gentlemen. Believe it or not, while the rule was met with some chagrin, there were no picket lines and no demonstrations or protest meetings. I would not have enjoyed what would have happened to me and my collegiate standing had we resorted to any such measures.

And now about the May Pole fight.

Not far from the southeast corner of the Campus, close to the banks of a small stream stood the Baughman Ice Cream factory. This institution manufactured a very good quality of frozen whole milk which they peddled about the streets of Topeka in small, horse drawn wagons. The horse's harness was equipped with a chime of bells and where ever this chime was heard in the offing the small fry hurried out with their money. They got a large scoop ladled out on a wooden plate which was commonly used as the container for the sale of bulk stored butter; and all this for a nickel. But the Baughman Brothers had another outlet. At the factory was a grove of trees and beneath them tables and benches. There you could and most of us did, wind up for refreshments after taking our lady for an evening buggy ride. They also had, to my recollection, the first drive in service, for they would serve you in your buggy if you wanted continued privacy.

On the morning of May 1st, 1901 the Freshman class, with the exception of the suicide squad which had carried the canes, assembled at the Ice Cream Factory. We reached there about 2:30 and waited for sunrise. I can well remember that day, waiting for the dawn, and with the class drawn closer together than at almost any other time.

At last, just at three o'clock the dark skies began to turn gray and the east to blush with pink.

At a signal, we all leaped up, carrying a puny pole we again cared nothing about, but making all the noise we could and yelling at the top of our voices. Hearing this the Sophomore class which had been awaiting us, started southeast from the chapel steps to intercept us, and as soon as they were well on their way the suicide boys who were lying in wait in the pine grove in front of Holbrook Hall, sprang into action. Before the Sophs could discover that they had been tricked again, the true pole was planted and solidly set in and we recorded another victory. There was enough violence as the aftermath of this defeat that the faculty again said never more, so the Cane Rush and the May Pole Fight died in each other's arms.

With them ended a colorful era of the college and to my own idea this was a distinct loss. These activities were school activities. The whole school participated. And they produced a united school front and a bond between students that I doubt the present sororities and frats can supply.

Up to my graduation the college had only one Greek letter association this was Tau Delta Pi, which still functions and was an honorary group of both men and women.

One other popular relaxation was an evening buggy ride with the young lady of your choice. Some of the students, like myself, had their own driving rigs, but if you didn't you could rent a single rig, rubber tired buggy and horse at a livery stable for $1.50 for five hours. There were drives about the country roads, and every week a band concert at Garfield Park at the extreme northern limit of North Topeka.

Much student activity also centered about the church and its many organizations. There were parties and other meetings, and then young men and women were expected to attend church; and there the boy and girl would work together. There wasn't much hint of anything ever wrong between a boy and girl who had attended worship together. But added to that it seems to me that while we had our sports and silly pranks, both sexes were far more mature than the college man or woman of today. They had been subject to the need for self control and for work for most of their lives, and all had a definite purpose in life. And college drop outs were few, and college morale high.

One of the favorite drives was out to Burnett's mound, a rather high and prominent hill a mile or so southwest of the college. This hill had been the home of an Indian named Burnett, though who owned it in my college days I do not know. One of the tragic things about Burnett's mound, was in its loss of tradition. It was firmly believed that no cyclone would ever devastate Topeka, since Burnett's mound was southwest of the town, and cyclones always came from the southwest and the mound would deflect it into the upper air and it would never touch Topeka. The tragic fact was that in 1966 a cyclone roared out of the southwest and in place of deflecting the gale it rolled down the side of the mound, destroying many of Washburn's buildings and in through the heart of Topeka, laying waste a wide path of death and devastation across the town.[16]

CHAPTER 13

The Era of Change

When I matriculated Washburn had a student body of around four hundred fifty in the college proper, together with another group in the Washburn Academy, who took little part in any college activity. But the student body was increasing, and the School of Law was opened in the fall of 1903, and the Kansas Medical College (which had helped organize the American Medical Association in 1890) was added with its building at Twelfth and Tyler and its student body.

When I entered College, it was my purpose to study medicine. I had never come into contact with courts or lawyers and never gave such a career a thought.

But early in my first year I began attending the First Presbyterian Church, along with numbers of my friends, and entered a young man's study class in Sunday School. This class was conducted by two Topeka lawyers, J. B. Larimore engaged in general practice and Nelson H. Loomis,[1] general attorney for Kansas for the Union Pacific railroad. In some way these men impressed me profoundly. Their attitude toward social problems and their idea of the Christian Man in public service were especially attractive. So suddenly I found myself in full swing for a legal education and the practice of the law.

At the time I made this decision I asked my friend and teacher N. H. Loomis, for permission to spend my summers in his office, reading law under his direction. This was the approved way at that time of entering the Bar.[2] The only law schools available were at the State Universities and some of the larger eastern schools. The permission granted I spent long summer days reading and having explained to me Kent's Commentaries and many other ponderous tomes. So when the opening of a law school was announced in 1903 I was anxious for immediate admittance.

The college had employed Ernest B. Conant[3] a member of the family in Massachusetts so long and so deeply involved in education, to act as the first Dean. As I look back now I can see him as a very young man on his first assignment, possessed of unusual administrative ability, a good personality and a beautiful baritone voice which he was not averse to displaying on invitation.

He organized his first faculty by getting the gratuitous help of several members of the Kansas Supreme Court and of the Shawnee County Bar. The ability of these men is well attested by the fact that in a few years Washburn obtained a wide reputation for its thoroughness and the breadth of its courses. One of the Supreme Court who taught, and who was always especially my ideal of a lawyer and a Judge was Henry Mason.[4] And his opinions were my guide in more ways than one. I well remember one lesson that he gave us was based on a case then pending but as yet undecided in the Supreme Court. We were each supposed to write our own opinion as we would if a member of that august body.

My work came back marked with the coveted "A"; which he explained to me after the case had finally been decided by the Court. "Well, your opinion didn't agree with the Court's, but you argued it out on the correct basis. I liked your reasoning even if I didn't agree. For remember this in nearly all appellate decisions, some one or more judges will dissent. Law is no hard and fast straight jacket. It is to be reasoned out; and if you reason well, you will in most cases reach a correct conclusion."

These men could have a tremendous influence on the young lawyer. I well remember the admonition of my preceptor N. H. Loomis: "Remember in all your practice that a poor settlement is far better than a good lawsuit." That seems to be more the method of present day lawyers than it really was at that time; when lawsuits raged over the most trivial of grievances; and the practice of law was more a game between rival members of the bar than a sincere endeavor to work out the conclusion which would do the most good and the least harm to all the litigants.

In order to enter the school that fall I made a deal with the school of arts faculty to carry my last two years of college along with my three years in law school, so that I didn't get my A.B. until 1905 rather than with the class of '04 with which I had been associated prior to that time. I finally did get the A.B. in 1905 without too much difficulty by spending a few less hours on amusements.

During my junior year I had met and become deeply attached to the co-ed who was later to become my wife, and the mother of my son Dwight who is now a member of the faculty of Harvard, with full professorship.[5] So during those last years, my living was divided at rather frantic speed between college, law school, paper route, and courtship. Neither seemed to suffer, though I was detained once after the class in logic by the teacher, who began with "Now I know the trouble you two young people are under, but I believe you'd both make better grades, if you'd move toward the front of the classroom, and get a bit further apart." Some way or other we made it. And I might add that on the founding of Tau Delta Pi, myself and Gertrude Ott were among the charter members. As for myself I always felt that my name was dropped in because they needed a few more names, but this was far from true with Gertrude.

The law school was opened on the upper floor of a business building on the north side of Eighth Street about half a block from Kansas Avenue. The beginnings were very modest, but also very adequate; and the enthusiasm of the young Dean fired the whole group.

There was a happening about this time in the strife torn nation of Mexico which aided all of us in the pursuit of knowledge.

Augustin Alba was a graduate of Chapultepec Military Academy which is the Mexican West Point, and was a general officer in the Mexican army, when there came one of those lightening revolutions and Augustin bet on the wrong horse, and had to get out of his homeland as fast as he could. He had no money, and no training other than military. But he did speak a little English and was a good cook. So he came to Topeka, where there was quite a little colony of Mexican workers with the Santa Fe Railroad. His business venture of opening a restaurant for Mexican foods in the first floor business section of the law school building was a lucky thing for him and for many of the students. For we could go to Augustin's and get a whopping bowl full of chili like nobody else ever was able to match, plus a bowl of Oyster crackers and a dip of chopped [onions] in vinegar for the total price of 5¢. Don't that sound ridiculous. But at that time money was money, and he made a success of his business at that rate. It's hard to calculate how many gallons of the product the students consumed; but I do know that my throat was so thoroughly cauterized that ever since the hottest of Mexican dishes held no terror for me. In fact I prefer them to the food of any other nation. So, so strange a thing as a Mexican Revolution can help a Kansas student.[6]

The Law School was started as a case book school. That is, very few actual texts were used. What we did was to read the opinions of appellate courts, analyze them and draw our own legal conclusions there from. That was rather a new and revolutionary method at that time; but it had one great advantage, the students learned how to examine the facts of any case presented to them, and evaluate the merits, rather than to try to apply some abstract rule, memorized from a text. We got to understand the reason of the rule and where it was applicable just as we would have to do later in our own offices when presented with the facts of a client's dilemma.[7]

Then too, there were constantly used a system of Mock Courts, where the student was given actual court room experience, under the supervision and criticism of capable and seasoned counsel.

My affairs moved along in even course, and nothing in particular happened except for the first flunk I ever obtained—it was in Bills and Notes and I had to put on a little extra pressure in an already full calendar to make it up. Then in the spring of 1905 I had a letter from an old and dear classmate of the academy days who had gone to the Indian Territory, been employed in a bank, and finally married the President's daughter. He held out to me glowing pictures of life in this last frontier, and begged me to come down and get admitted to the bar and practice in his town; promising me active support of the bank in business affairs.

Well, I felt at that time that what I wanted most was to be admitted and start practicing. For the first time in my life I let impatience govern my actions. But as I said later, at that time I was more interested in the degree P.F. (Pater Familias)[8] than that of Ll.B.[9] So I began to make my plans accordingly.

I felt I could pass any reasonable bar examination and that by March 1906, I would have completed all the courses of which I had need, and all I would miss would be the actual commencement and conferring of the degree. I failed to see that later I would regret the failure to complete the final year, and know full well that I could have done as well at my new location had I waited the thing out. As it was I made arrangements to take a bar examination in the Federal District Court at Okmulgee, I.T.[10] This Court held written examinations at stated intervals and there was a large group of incoming lawyers young and old who took it with me.

Okmulgee was the Capital of the Creek Nation, one of the five civilized tribes of which I wrote earlier. The Council House which was the tribal Capital Building and Court House stood at the center of town, in a large Court House Square. It was a building of gray stone, ample for all the uses for which it was needed.

At that time, the Indian Territory was still under Federal jurisdiction, the Courts were all Federal Courts, and the life of the citizens was continually affected by federal laws, and by the rules and conduct of federal boards and bureaus. At that time the National Government was firmly entrenched Republicanism. Knowing this I secured a letter of introduction from Hon. Chas. Curtis who was then the Chairman of [the] Indian Affairs Committee of the House of Representatives. Mr. Curtis and I became acquainted in some of his political campaigns, for I had always taken part in such events; and I had read law a short time with Hib Case, the Topeka lawyer who had been the Congressman's partner before he entered Congress.[11]

I arrived at Okmulgee at the appointed time and went to the Council House and reported to the examiners. At the same time I sent my letter from Congressman Curtis to the Judge in his chambers, as the required proof of my impeccable moral worth.

It was a written examination, and was plenty tough, but about two in the afternoon the door to the passage way that led to Chambers was opened by a benign gentleman, with long white beard, and garbed in the Prince Albert coat then the stigma of a judge.

This gentleman, speaking with a pronounced German accent said, "Vill de young chentleman who hat de letter from Congressman Curtis please come into my chanber."

I complied with great fear and trepidation, to be greeted graciously and invited to a chair.

"Chust how vell do you know Congressman Curtis, young man?" he asked. And I explained our acquaintance and how well we had known each other. Then came the most glorious statement human ears ever heard.

"Young man. We in de Indian Territory know Mr. Curtis. He does many ting for us. When you go back tell Mr. Curtis what we tink of him here, how ve admire and appreciate him. And young man DOOON' YOU VORRY ABOUT DE EXAMINATION."

To this day, I don't know whether I passed the examination or whether I was admitted to the bar because I had a nice letter from Congressman Curtis.[12]

This may seem strange to you, and of course it was a bit unusual. But I grew to have a very deep affection for this old Judge. He found that I was able to speak German, and after that when [we] were met on Circuit I had to eat at his table, and share with him some of his special rye bread or other delicacy. Some called him tyrant, I never called him anything other than friend.

The examination was in October 1905 and my admittance to the bar almost to the day, 62 years ago, from this day in October 1967, when I am now writing.

After I received my license to practice before the Federal Courts, I went back to Washburn and stayed in class until the end of the mid year session, then went to Weleetka, a country town about forty miles south of Okmulgee and opened my office as a practicing lawyer.

In 1905 the laws necessary to the admittance of the Indian Territory had all been enacted. It had been finally determined that the two Territories, Oklahoma and Indian Territory must be admitted as one state rather than two. Quite an effort had been made to gain admittance of the Indian Territory as the State of Sequoyah, after the great Cherokee scholar and statesman who had produced an alphabet in which the Cherokee tongue could be written. But there was the great additional expense which would be involved in two separate state governments, and a far more cogent reason, there was every reason to expect that this area would be strongly democrat, and it was far better for a Republican to have only two new democratic senators, rather than four.[13]

But the passage of the enabling act forced the new state to set up a legislative assembly to draft a new Constitution, and to divide the new state into Counties and Congressional Districts. This was to be my principal interest for the time that I spent at Weleetka.

CHAPTER 14

The Birth of a New Commonwealth

When I reached Weleetka and opened my office the fires were just beginning to burn. Naturally every town of any consequence wished the new counties to be shaped so that they would be the logical county seat. The result would well spell the continued growth or the ultimate stagnation. Near Weleetka two other towns, Henrietta and Okemah, with Weleetka were the active contenders.

One who has never gone through these county seat fights can[not] have much of a conception of what it meant. The participants felt that they were struggling for survival, and any means, trickery, violence, outright bribery were legitimate tools, for this life and death struggle.

Of course I was plummeted right into the middle of things in support of my hometown.

As I told you previously, the Indian Territory was dependent upon the Federal Government for its laws, its officers and whatever of patronage there might be. Since the Government was Republican, the man who hoped for any patronage, had to appear Republican too.[1] That brought about the fact that the local paper was Republican in policy while its editor was a hide bound Georgia Democrat, than which there were none other more partisan. Sensing that in our county seat fight, since most of the citizens actually were members of the Democrat persuasion, a paper of the same creed might well prove useful, and hearing that I had some experience in newspaper work during my college and law school days, he came to me with the strangest proposal. He stated that he had ample equipment to set up another paper, and that if I would edit and publish a Democratic sheet he would divide his shop and set me up and help me all he could.

This proposal was so unusual and offered such opportunities for gaining an acquaintance over the area that I took it up, and from that day on the Georgia Democrat published a rip roaring Republican paper; while I, a dyed in the wool, born, bred and reared Republican of the type that at the present time would be called Barry Goldwater,[2] did the same for a Democrat paper. One thing we were both in a position to know the weaknesses of his opponent; though we kept a friendly face and pushed county seat day in and day out.

My office equipment was ample but rather primitive. We printed our paper on a big Gordon jobber, manipulated by treadle power furnished by the editor and his able assistant. The assistant was a Creek boy about twenty-five, named Running Deer. He had developed an accomplishment of which he was inordinately proud, he could take his pen and sign his name by drawing at one sweep, without lifting his pen from the paper, a picture of a running deer, antlers and all. But don't picture this man as a crude savage. The fact is he was for the time and place extremely well educated and was a thorough gentleman. One of his accomplishments on the physical side was to stand behind the big press and once it was in motion to ease the task of treadling by pumping up and down on a cross bar at the back of the press.

Of course all our news was hand set, and to save work and fill space we used a paper that was called "patent," which had one side preprinted with general news and the advertisement of Lydia Pinkham, the Smith Brothers and the like.[3] The company who furnished the paper were paid by the advertisers and so could let us have it at a price we could afford to pay. Also we always carried what was called "Boiler plate," which were advertisements and filler articles ready set on a slab of type metal which we could set in any space for which we had no news of our own.

The fight for the county seat grew so hot that there were frequent threats of vengeance from the other two towns. I was duly warned that if I didn't end my articles in support of Weleetka that I would be shot and my paper burned. This was the one and only time in my life I ever had more in my hip pocket than a handkerchief; and what I'd have done with that thirty-two[4] if I had been called upon to use it is hard to guess. At any rate, Running Deer and I let it be generally known that we were ready for any action needed, and the matter was never more than a threat.

Weleetka was in the center of what later became the great Oklahoma oil fields. At this time there were abortive attempts to establish corporations for prospecting and buying lands for exploration; but no one on the spot, as is always the case, had any idea that there was anything to the idea. It was just another promoter's scheme to bilk the people out of the hard earned savings. One company did open an office in Weleetka. It was called the Iowa Trust Company and was a land buying organization. I moved my offices into the suite they occupied and together with the local representative, handled numerous land transactions.

One such transaction which I had cause to remember was in the purchase of a forty acre tract from a negro woman registered as a Creek full blood. This woman lived at a small whistle stop the first town west of Weleetka and what was specially interesting to me was that this village was entirely negro. Negro store keepers, officials and business men, and a white man, while welcome in daytime if he had any business to attend to, after sundown he must be gone. There were several such small towns in Oklahoma, a sort of segregation in the reverse. The agent of the company who had consummated the sale had offered the owner four hundred dollars, which was extra high for the land involved and she was delighted with her good fortune. I made out the deed and she signed it and I then took her acknowledgement, and after wandering about the village, caught a train back home. I never anticipated hearing of this transaction again, when, to my surprise, in 1938 I received a subpoena from the Federal Court at Tulsa, Oklahoma to appear and testify in an action between two larger oil companies, one of whom claimed this land by deed from the buyer and the other who claimed as the heirs of the negro woman, claiming that she was mentally unbalanced and that the deed was fraudulent. It seems that after the death of the negro woman, a rival company wanting this particular land, had hunted up her heirs and bought from them and now were demanding possession and an accounting. That accounting would have been painful for, since the deed, over four million dollars' worth of oil had been extracted from that forty [acres]. After hearing all the evidence the Court promptly decided for the claimant under the deed.[5] And in truth, that woman was just as sane as any person living and was tickled pink to get what she thought was about twice what the old woods forty was worth. But that is the history of all such developments; the native seldom reaps any of the benefits. He is of little faith in what he knows so well and can't see any chance of improvement.

With all these things moving and so many irons in the fire, we decided to build us a home. It was deep in the woods about a half mile from the main part of town, just a trail through the fields to reach it; and it was just a little bungalow type place, that looked more or less like a hat box when compared to the huge oak trees which towered about it, many of them waving in their branches big bunches of mistletoe. But it was a home and it was all ours and we were very happy. My wife was a very talented musician, and the one luxury that we brought with us from Topeka was a new piano. It was very wonderful for me to sit outside the house of a warm afternoon or evening, while she, within, played melodies that blended in perfection with the wind sighing through the upper branches of the trees.

Practice in that place was apt to have its startling moments. I was called on to visit and consult with a man who lived about six miles out of town, at a place where there was a blacksmith shop and country store. I hired me a good saddle horse and set out to answer his summons. He was supposed to meet me at the store and when he didn't appear, I asked the store keeper if he had seen him and when he said yes, I asked him if he had left any message for me. To this he replied no, but that if I wanted to see him I'd find him in the smoke house at the back of the store. I did. But we had no consultation. My man was lying composedly on his back with a neat, round bullet hole, smack between his eyes. I asked the store keeper about it, and he said it was the man's fault in pushing another too far; and as to telling me, he just wanted to see what my reaction would be. Well, I went back and put the horse rental into the expense column with regret. Money was never any too plentiful.

The Indians of the five tribes were an intensely religious people though that religion in its functioning had some odd aspects. They were almost to a man Baptists of the primitive hard shell type.[6] And their worship confused in many ways with old taboos and beliefs. The five tribes were called civilized, because they were already attached to the soil, not nomads like the western tribes; and had extensive towns and permanent farms. Their homes were well built and comfortable. And their capabilities great. They were a prosperous, healthy lot, and living in comparative peace as a civilized community. This until the white man coveted their lands, and then all treaties with them became scraps of paper, and they were driven out. But they carried many of their customs with them.

One of the customs was to connect their church worship with a dance. On Saturday afternoon the farm wagons from all about would meet and center at the church house. All came prepared to camp for the night. On Saturday night there was the stomp dance. A circle about fifty feet in diameter was worn hard as a brick, and utterly devoid of vegetation of any kind. You would find these stomp grounds at every meeting house and often at other convenient spots in the forest. Decked in tribal regalia the dancers would fasten on each ankle empty clam shells, filled with pebbles and carry in their hands large gourd rattles also with its pebbles. The dance was a circling affair, with stomping, shaking of rattles at foot and hand, accompanied by posturing in age dictated patterns and the whole sounded off to the tune of yells, shouts and screams and the monotony of the drums. They would keep this din and dancing up until completely exhausted; sleep until morning, then attend what some times were all day religious meetings and depart for home, cheered, up to date on local news, and with all sincerity feeling themselves cleansed and forgiven. And I rather think The Great Spirit accepted them with a bit more pleasure than with more sophisticated worshipers. They believed what they did was right and it was done with all their heart, mind and strength. Too often the so called wiser worshipers carry with them into the sanctuary, feelings and desires, thoughts and attitudes which they carry out with them, no better a man than when they entered.

One thing that made practice of the law in Indian Territory anything but a pleasure were the laws under which we were compelled to proceed. It came about in one of those odd and peculiar political accomplishments that always seem to be crowding into our affairs.

It so happened that the State of Arkansas in 1845 printed a lot more of their laws than they could dispose of and there was a whole basement of these 1845 Arkansas law books in the Capital Building at Little Rock. Then the Arkansas Delegation in Congress had an inspiration. They got Congress without even its usual minimum of thinking, to adopt these Arkansas Laws as the governing law of the Indian Territory.[7] And here all at once the State of Arkansas was in the book business and the old white elephant became a valuable asset. And here we were, practicing under the old English common law procedure, three quarters of a century after it had become obsolete in every other place. That certainly was a stroke of genius on the part of the Arkansas delegation, but it condemned us lawyers to wander forever in the maze of petitions, replies, replications, surreplications, rebutter and surrebutter and all the rest which made the English law until code pleading was adopted, a complete nightmare to a lawyer who wanted to get his case tried in the most sensible way and with the greatest expedition.

Now the climax of all our efforts was at hand. The arguments that had been hurtling back and forth all spring and summer, now came to the testing ground. Election systems were outlined and provisions were made for the calling of necessary meetings, and locations were set for the holding of local elections to choose delegates to the Constitutional Convention which would write the basic law of the new state. Since one of the first functions of this Constitutional Convention was the locating of the boundaries and the naming of the County Seats in the new counties, control of this convention or at least of the local representation was vital. Our area was to hold its convention at Okemah, one of the rival towns, which didn't exactly please us; but there was no escape. So on the appointed day the delegates from each of the three towns met and assembled as specified. The delegates who had been locally chosen for this meeting were equally divided between the three towns, so as a first move, Weleetka and Okemah combined to elect me chairman of the convention and thus remove one Weleetka delegate from the floor and prevent his taking part in the discussions.

That strategy worked very well so far, but as the delegates were equally divided between the towns, the alliance when it came actually to voting, fell wholly apart and no one had a majority, because Weleetka would not join with either [of] the other two and without her no majority was possible for either one without a defection of an opponent's own delegate.

And so we sat, and wrangled for the better part of the day. They tossed my way every sort of notion that the human mind could conceive. They tried to adjourn until another day. Every trick and subterfuge imaginable, but again, the group was so divided, that when any one group tried to appeal from the chair the other two gave the chair a majority. Finally along toward the latter part of the afternoon, after a short recess when we came back and another vote was called for, two members of the Weleetka delegation switched and voted for the Okemah slate. This gave Okemah a working plurality, but to make it sure we didn't have a chance, Henrietta turned its whole delegation to Okemah and the job was done. With deep regret, I packaged, signed and sealed the voting sheets and the complete returns, and sent them on their way, and we returned home a sadly disappointed and disgusted group. One of the men who switched to Okemah was a lawyer, who immediately pulled up stakes and moved to Tulsa. The other was a real estate man who was an insignificant nonentity, and who we believed had received only a small part of the payoff which we were sure had been the reason for the switch. But townsmen didn't think enough of him to be even too resentful.

With county seat hopes gone, I knew that if I intended to practice law I would probably have to move to the County seat; and this didn't seem to me too practical a step. For I had fought so hard for Weleetka that I had made enemies of about all the people in the two other communities and I feared my practice would be about nil. Then too, the glamour of the new state was gone and the new conditions were unattractive. The country was on a one crop cotton basis, and no one had any money save at cotton picking time; when they went to the store and turned in their cotton and had it applied on the bill they had run the previous year. Frequently it was not enough to clear up the whole bill, so a new credit year had to be started with the farmer already in debt for the arrears, so that he was practically in peonage to the store keeper for another year. He could sell his cotton only to the store that held the mortgage, and was unable to take advantage of any bargains elsewhere. Since the farmer couldn't get any money except at picking time, unless he borrowed it at the store and had it put on his bill, the lawyer, the doctor, and all else were about as badly off as any other for ready money. That is the curse of King Cotton, which has kept his subjects in ignorance and poverty all over the cotton raising areas even to this day. But hard as that system was, the average farmer who knew nothing else, had to plod on in his weary way, earning what he could and living as best he might. The tragedy of the south is that progress in farming there has only made matters worse for the average farm worker. Mechanization has driven him from even such poor jobs as his hard way of life provided, and he has migrated to the cities where his present lot is worse than the former.

My personal situation was not too bad. I still had friends among the lawyers and the fellow citizens of Topeka and I began making plans for my return to take up my practice there. I was fortunate in getting things satisfactorily arranged, so I turned my printing plant back to the owner, and started north.

CHAPTER 15

Journey's End

As the day hand of the years crept further round the dial of the century, one could begin to sense the ending of an era, an era beyond which I do not propose this tale to go.

I opened my office and commenced to practice, and was blessed with reasonable success; not near the successes of my dreams, yet not nearly as bad as it might have been. But much as I loved my profession and enjoyed the challenge of each action, still the attitude of it all was different.

Paul Bunyan had retreated into some distant mountain and men were proceeding to grind Old Blue up into hamburger. The heroes were passing. True, Chalky Beason, the old Dodge City Saloon keeper was still coming to take his seat in the Kansas Legislature every biennium.[1] True, Bat Masterson was still Marshal in Oklahoma.[2] True, Bud Ledbetter another old time Kansas lawman served as deputy in the eastern half of the state.[3] Buffalo Bill had his wild west troupe continually on the road. But then he was never really anything more than a butcher turned showman. All he ever did as to the Buffalo was to slaughter them for the railroads to feed their construction crews. His life after that was obscure until his spurious fame was used by the penny dreadful writers to fill their lurid magazines.[4] Most of the plainsmen had ridden over their last horizon, and what few were left were fighting arthritis in place of Indians and finding it a more savage and relentless foe.

The only ones left were the few who had been quite young when the buffalo herds still had their great migrations and it is of one of these I'd like to tell you, to show that decency and gentleness had as great a play in the days of the western march as at any other era.

One day there walked into my office, a tall, erect elderly gentleman, impeccably dressed, and carrying a wide brimmed horseman's hat in his hand. He introduced himself to me as Charles Jones, and stated his business which I undertook. He remained my client as long as I stayed in Topeka, and I came to know him intimately. To my surprise when I learned his true identity, he was Buffalo Charley Jones, and far more entitled to that prefix than ever was Cody.[5]

As a young man of 17 Charley had left his home in an older state and started to earn his fortune in the west. That was the era of the hide hunter, the most disgraceful era in many ways of the taming of the west. The demand for a buffalo coat or a buffalo robe sent the prices skyrocketing, and hordes of human vultures scattered over the plains, killing the magnificent beasts of the great migrations by the thousands. A hunting crew was usually made up of numerous mounted killers accompanying a grub and supply wagon and one or more hide wagons operated by one or more skinners. When the herd was located the hunters started out on its flank shooting and shooting and leaving the bodies of their victims strung out behind them. The skinners would drive the wagon along the kill, strip off the hides and leave the carcass to rot as it lay. Small wonder that the plains Indians who had depended on these migrations for the supplying of their food and clothing needs, looked with horror on such useless waste. So thickly were these carcasses left that for years other scavengers earned a living by following the same trail and gathering the whitened bones for shipment east.

One can well understand the desire for a buffalo pelt. You have never felt comfort until you have ridden in a sleigh in zero temperature wrapped snuggly in a buffalo robe; or lain as a child on a buffalo robe in front of the fire place. Bedrooms in those days were unheated, and I have a clear memory how as a little boy, I would snuggle down in bed with that robe tossed over me, and defy winter to do its worst. The skins were rather harshly haired at first appearance, but under those coarse outer hairs lay a pelt of softest wool, delightful to the touch. There were many uses for the skins. One was to cut a head hole in the center and drape it over the shoulders like a poncho.

Charley Jones joined a hide hunter outfit, but the useless slaughter disgusted and sickened him, and he soon sought other employment. He saw what no one else even considered or dreamed, that the big herds would in a few more years be totally extinct. So he started hunting in another way. He managed to get a body of land together partly owned and under his control and went to hunting buffalo with a lasso in place of a gun. The buffalo calves he caught were transported to this ranch, and his herd grew great and strong. And it came to pass that Charley Jones' herd contained all the buffalo left in the United States. There was another small herd which had escaped into western Canada; and every buffalo today is descended from the offspring of Charley's herd and the Canadian. If you see a buffalo; or if you taste the sweetness of a hump steak, you just stop and realize that save for Charley Jones those great beasts would have faded into history with the carrier pigeon and the other native life that the white man in his wanton waste of nature, destroyed.

So I still assert that Charley Jones is far more entitled to the prefix "Buffalo" before his name than Bill Cody. The only difference was that Bill Cody was a wanton show off, and Charley Jones was a quiet, unassuming gentleman, who regarded his act as the most ordinary of action one might take.

The struggle from now on, was to be a contest in the market place, or the field of politics, where then, as now, the aim might be high but the means were frequently very dubious.

There were no more new lands to conquer. There were no more flamboyant adventures to be had. Men ceased to be heroes and became hum drum ordinary men. The Grand Army of the Republic, which from the civil war until near the end of the first decade of the twentieth century had dominated Kansas politics was beginning bitterly to thin out. They were now in their old age willing to accept the pension which in their sturdy youth they had rejected with scorn. I actually know how some of them would react to the offer of a pension, with the answer "I'm no damn government pauper." But every year the encampment called fewer and fewer participants, and soon had become mostly a memory. Writers with no knowledge had written slanderous and utterly untrue descriptions of the western life, so that the whole world, eager to accept sensationalism, had people[d] the west with gun slingers and outlaws who never existed and beat them down with impossible heroes who set in saloons, conducted by lovely ladies and swilled down whiskey without a chaser in sufficient quantities of an evening to put him not under the table but under the sod. The West was colorful enough with the true heroes who fought insect and drought, cyclone and blizzard, depressions and panics and came up smiling and asking for more, and in the end created an empire far larger and richer than Alexander's. Some poet, I can't remember his name, expressed the change far better than I can when he sang:

I fancied that romance was dead;
That knighthood was no more;
Instead of brave old songs I heard
The streets incessant roar;
The days of knight and chevalier
Were o'er forever o'er.
I looked from your dear eyes, sweetheart
Back to the world, and then
I saw romance in the lofty walls
And knights in busy men;
And through the roar I heard
The dear old minstrelsy again.

It is always a bit sad in parting with old friends; even though we know such partings are inevitable. And so we look back to "The dear dead days beyond recall"[6] with a feeling of loss. And truly much has been lost but too, much has been gained. That is the way of all growth.

Romance is not dead. There are still dragons to slay; and they still breathe destruction, though in another form. And praise God, there are still Americans who will accept the challenge.

And now, good night dear friends. You can claim no higher honor, there is no higher citation, than to be called "Sons of the pioneers."

FINIS

Notes

Introduction

1. A. J. Bolinger to Dwight Bolinger, October 27, 1967, copy of letter in editor's possession.

2. A. J. Bolinger was appointed judge of the probate and magistrate courts by Republican Missouri governor Forrest C. Donnell in 1941. He was elected to the position in 1942 and was reelected until the late 1960s. Bruce Bolinger to Jeffrey H. Barker, September 3, 2009, letter in editor's possession.

3. For work on the history of childhood, see Steven Mintz, *Huck's Raft: A History of American Childhood* (Cambridge, MA: Harvard University Press, 2004); Kriste Lindemeyer, *The Greatest Generation Grows Up: American Childhood in the 1930s* (Chicago: Dee, 2005); James Martin, *Children and Youth in a New Nation* (New York: New York University Press, 2009); and Pamela Riney-Kehrberg, *Childhood on the Farm: Work, Play, and Coming of Age in the Midwest* (Lawrence: University Press of Kansas, 2005).

4. Ingalls quoted in Craig Miner, *Kansas: The History of the Sunflower State, 1854–2000* (Lawrence: University Press of Kansas, 2002), 3; *New York Times* quoted in Scott G. McNall, *The Road to Rebellion: Class Formation and Kansas Populism, 1865–1900* (Chicago: University of Chicago Press, 1988), 63.

5. Details of early Kansas history are drawn from Miner, *Kansas: The History*; H. Craig Miner and William E. Unrau, *The End of Indian Kansas: A Study of Cultural Revolution* (Lawrence: Regents Press of Kansas, 1978); Paul Wallace Gates, *Fifty Million Acres: Conflicts over Kansas Land Policy, 1854–1890* (New York: Atherton, 1966); James R. Shortridge, *Peopling the Plains: Who Settled Where in Frontier Kansas* (Lawrence: University Press of Kansas, 1995); Peter Iverson, "Native Peoples and Histories," and David J. Weber, "The Spanish-Mexican Rim," both in Clyde A. Milner II, Carol A. O'Connor, and Martha A. Sandweiss, eds., *The Oxford History of the American West* (New York: Oxford University Press, 1994), 13–78.

6. Miner, *Kansas: The History*, 33–35.

7. Shortridge, *Peopling the Plains*, 1; Miner, *Kansas: The History*, 49–55, 64.

8. Quoted in Miner, *Kansas: The History*, 100.

9. Information on William Bolinger drawn from US Census of Population, 1860, Place: Sharpsburg, Washington, Maryland; Roll: M653_483; Page: 0; Image: 258 and 1870, Census Place: Springfield, Sangamon, Illinois; Roll: M593_282; Page: 507; Image: 417; and Kansas Marriage Index, 1854–73 (database on-line). Provo, UT: Generations Network, Inc., 1998, www.ancestry.com, accessed July 16, 2008. Some records refer to Delia as Ada Delia and others as Amanda Delia.

10. Biographical information on Joel Hostetter from Cutler, http://www.kancoll.org/books/cutler/elk/elk-co-p9.html#LONGTON, accessed April 28, 2020; US Census of Population 1860, Place: Perry, Noble, Indiana; Roll: M653_285; Page: 105; Image: 106; and 1870, Place: Ottawa Ward 2, Franklin, Kansas; Roll: M593_434; Page: 137; Image: 277, www.Ancestry.com, July 16, 2008; and *Kansas State Census Collection, 1855–1915* (database on-line). Provo, UT: Generations Network, Inc., 2007; www.Ancestry.com, accessed July 16, 2008.

11. Figures from the 1880 Census of Population retrieved from Historical Census Browser, University of Virginia, Geospatial and Statistical Data Center, http://fisher.lib.virginia.edu/collections/stats/histcensus/index.html, accessed July 18, 2008.

12. Data on the history of Elk County and Longton drawn from Frank W. Blackmar, ed., *Kansas: A Cyclopedia of State History, Embracing Events, Institutions, Industries, Counties, Cities, Towns, Prominent Persons, etc. vol. III* (Chicago: Standard Pub. Co., 1912), 187, transcribed July 2002 by Carolyn Ward, http://www.ksgenweb.org/archives/1912/b/blackmar_frank_wilson.html, accessed April 28, 2020; William G. Cutler, *History of the State of Kansas* (Chicago: A. T. Andreas, 1883), http://www.kancoll.org/books/cutler/elk/elk-co-p2.html, accessed April 28, 2020.

13. Rainfall figures from McNall, *Road to Rebellion*, 66.

14. McNall, 69–75; Miner, 23–28.

15. Corn price data from McNall, *Road to Rebellion*, 3, 78.

16. McNall, 75–79; Miner, *Kansas: The History*, 138–141; Allan G. Bogue, "An Agricultural Empire," in Milner et al., *Oxford History*, 294.

17. McNall, 82; Miner, *Kansas: The History*, 139–143.

18. Miner, *Kansas: The History*, 141–146; McNall, *Road to Rebellion*, 43–44.

19. McNall, 45–60; Miner, *Kansas: The History*, 172–176.

20. McNall, *Road to Rebellion*, 45.

21. Lease quoted in McNall, 4; Miner, *Kansas: The History*, 179; Harriet Sigerman, "Laborers for Liberty, 1865–1890," in Nancy Cott, ed., *No Small Courage: A History of Women in the United States* (New York: Oxford University Press, 2000), 337.

22. Miner, *Kansas: The History*, 182–187.

23. See Erich Rauchway, *Murdering McKinley: The Making of Theodore Roosevelt's America* (New York: Hill and Wang, 2003), 155–159.

24. Miner, *Kansas: The History*, 156. For more on the temperance movement, see Janet Giele, *Two Paths to Women's Equality: Temperance, Suffrage, and the Origins of Modern Feminism* (New York: Twayne, 1995) and Jean H. Baker, *Sisters: The Lives of America's Suffragists* (New York: Hill and Wang, 2005).

25. Information on Southern Kansas Academy from Kansas State Historical Society, *The Columbian History of Education in Kansas* (Topeka: Hamilton Printing Company, 1893), https://www.google.com/books/edition/Columbian_History_of_Education_in_Kansas/iIHfAAAAMAAJ?hl=en&gbpv=1&dq=inauthor:%22Board+of+directors+of+the+Kansas+educational+exhibit%22&printsec=frontcover, accessed April 28, 2020; the papers of Bishop John Gregg, Kenneth Spencer Research Library, University of Kansas, https://archives.lib.ku.edu/repositories/3/resources/3412, accessed April 28, 2020.

26. "Our Washburn," history of Washburn University, https://www.washburn.edu/about/facts/History/index.html, accessed April 28, 2020.

27. See "Prohibition," Kansas Historical Society, https://www.kshs.org/kansapedia/prohibition/14523, accessed April 28, 2020; Pete Dulin, *Kansas City Beer: A History of Brewing in the Heartland* (Charleston, SC: American Palate/History Press, 2016).

28. Kenny A. Franks and Paul F. Lambert, *Oklahoma: The Land and Its People* (Helena, MT: American and World Geographic, 1994), 13, 17–31; Bonnie Lynn-Sherow, *Red Earth: Race and Agriculture in Oklahoma Territory* (Lawrence: University Press of Kansas, 2004), 6–25.

29. Franks and Lambert, *Oklahoma*, quote on p. 30; Clyde A. Milner II, "National Initiatives," in Milner et al., *Oxford History*, 155–194; Jeanne Boydston, Nick Cullather, Jan Ellen Lewis, Michael McGerr, and James Oakes, *Making a Nation: The United States and Its People* (Saddle River, NJ: Prentice-Hall, 2002), 505. For further discussion of the modification and consequences of the Dawes Act, see chapter 10, note 2.

30. Lynn-Sherow, *Red Earth*, 26–30; Franks and Lambert, *Oklahoma*, 30; and Milner et al., *Oxford History*, 184–191.

31. Milner et al., 191.

32. Weleetka history from "Stories of Early Oklahoma: A Collection of Interesting Facts, Biographical Sketches and Stories Relating to the History of Oklahoma." Assembled by Hazel Ruby McMahan (Mrs. James W.), State Historian for Oklahoma Society Daughters of American Revolution (1945), Okfuskee County Archives, http://files.usgwarchives.net/ok/okfuskee/history/town/howele01.txt, accessed April 28, 2020.

33. See chapter 15, p. 141; and Arthur Joel Bolinger, "A. J. Bolinger Reminisces," audio recording in editors' possession.

34. See, for example, *Anderson v. Board of Commissioners of Shawnee County* 91 Kan. 362, 137 P. 799 (January 10, 1914), a 1914 case in which A. J. attempted, unsuccessfully, to secure witness fees for a police officer testifying in court.

35. Arthur Joel Bolinger, "A. J. Bolinger Reminisces," audio recording in editors' possession; on the Army Trials and Wright's flight, see http://memory.loc.gov/ammem/wrighthtml/wrighttime2.html, accessed April 28, 2020.

36. See *Kansas State Census Collection, 1855–1915* (database on-line). Provo, UT: Generations Network, Inc., 2007, accessed September 2, 2009; also, letter from A. J. Bolinger to Bruce Bolinger, May 15, 1950, original letter in possession of Bruce Bolinger.

37. Arthur Joel Bolinger, "A. J. Bolinger Reminisces," audio recording in editors' possession. Source for the record of the marriage of A. J. Bolinger and Ella B. Harrison: Marriage Licenses, State of Missouri, County of Ralls, www.ancestry.com, accessed August 25, 2009.

38. Mary Julia Bolinger Barker, interviewed by Jeff Barker, August 30, 2009, Greenville, SC, notes in editors' possession.

39. Arthur Joel Bolinger, "A. J. Bolinger Reminisces," audio recording in editors' possession.

40. Arthur Joel Bolinger, *Mine Eyes Unto the Hills* (New York: Vantage, 1966); see also John Wesley Hall, "A Glance at Readin' an' Ritin' in the Ozarks," *OzarksWatch* 8, no. 3 (1995), https://thelibrary.org/lochist/periodicals/ozarkswatch/ow8031.htm, accessed April 28, 2020.

41. Miner, *Kansas: The History*, 126–127, 164–168; Julie Roy Jeffrey, *Frontier Women: The Trans-Mississippi West, 1840–1880* (New York: Hill and Wang, 1979), esp. 12–19, 50, 73–79.

42. Jeffrey, 79–85, quote on 12.

43. Mary Julia Bolinger Barker, interviewed by Melissa Walker and Jeff Barker, November 3, 2006, Greenville, SC, tape and transcript in editors' possession.

44. Indeed, Mari Sandoz received a letter from her father in 1926, after Mari had become a writer, telling her that "you know I consider writers and

artists the maggots of society." See Mari Sandoz, *Old Jules* (Lincoln: University of Nebraska Press, 1962). The passage from the letter from Jules Sandoz to his daughter is found in the introduction by Linda M. Hasselstrom.

Chapter One: Background in General

1. Longton, KS, is located in the southeast corner of the state, at the meeting of Hitchin Creek and the Elk River. Two lines of the Atchison, Topeka & Santa Fe Railroad (merged with the Burlington Northern Railroad in 1996 to form the Burlington Northern and Santa Fe Railway) met at Longton. The town was founded in 1870 as Elk Rapids.

2. The need for western cattle in eastern US markets during and after the Civil War created both pressure and opportunity for settlement in Kansas. Prior to 1867, Kansas law prohibited the driving of Texas cattle through Kansas in summer. This was due to the danger of Texas cattle fever, an infectious tick-borne illness of the blood (caused by the protozoan *Babesia bigemina* or *Babesia bovis*), which had spread to and killed large numbers of cattle from Oklahoma, Kansas, Missouri, and northward. The law was revised in 1867 to allow cattle to be driven into southwest Kansas, west of the Sixth Principal Meridian, which ran west of Longton. The importance of the cattle industry was such that railroad construction and investment and thus settlement followed the location of the terminus for cattle drives at Abilene, and later in Ellsworth, Wichita, and other towns. See J. L. Stratton, *Pioneer Women: Voices from the Kansas Frontier* (New York: Touchstone, 1982), 206–208; C. K. Hutson, "Texas Cattle Fever in Kansas, 1866–1930," *Agricultural History* 6, no. 1 (Winter 1994): 74–104; and J. Gray, *Desperate Seed: Ellsworth, Kansas on the Violent Frontier* (N.p.: Kansas Cowboy Publications, 2009), 6f.

3. One "hand" equals four inches; thus, a horse fourteen hands high would stand fifty-six inches at the withers (that is, measuring from the bottom of the hoof to the junction of the neck and the back).

4. In cattle drives, the horse-mounted drovers assigned to the "drag" position are at the rear of the herd, preventing stragglers from being separated from the herd.

5. That is, the fire and stink of hell. See Isaiah 30:33. The biblical reference is to a valley southeast of Jerusalem, place of child sacrifice to Moloch; later, a place of torment and the burning of corpses.

6. Miss Kitty Russell was a character played by actress Amanda Blake (1929–1989) on the CBS television series, *Gunsmoke*, from 1955–1974. The series ran for one additional year.

7. Apparently this is a reference to Dr. Mary Edwards Walker, a New Yorker who received her medical degree from Syracuse University in 1855.

Walker became an early proponent of dress reform for women. Amelia Bloomer devised ruffled pants to be worn under skirts that came down to a woman's mid-calf, known as bloomers, and in her early years of medical practice, Dr. Walker wore bloomers. Later, she wore men's-style suits. Some sources claim that Walker was arrested more than once for wearing pants. Walker went on to serve as a surgeon in the Union Army during the Civil War. She was awarded the Medal of Honor for her service. See Kerry Gleason, Nancy Osborne, and Ed Vermue, "Mary Edwards Walker, M.D.: A Bibliography," http://www.oswego.edu/library/archives/walker.pdf, accessed May 4, 2020.

8. According to Kansas historian R. Alton Lee, early Kansas also attempted to regulate the length of bedsheets and to ban mincemeat. See R. Alton Lee, "The 'Little White Slaver' in Kansas," *Kansas History* 22, no. 4 (Winter 1999/2000): 58–267, http://www.kshs.org/publicat/history/1999 winter_lee.pdf, accessed May 4, 2020.

9. Kansas preceded federal prohibition of alcohol by nearly forty years. The National Prohibition Act of 1919 (the Volstead Act) went into effect in February 1920; Kansas enacted prohibition in 1880. Governor John P. St. John headed a successful effort to amend the state constitution through a ballot initiative. St. John ran for president of the United States in 1884 as the Prohibition Party candidate, losing to Grover Cleveland.

While the Volstead Act was repealed in 1933, Kansas retained statewide prohibition until 1948. See Robert Smith Bader, *Prohibition in Kansas: A History* (Lawrence: University Press of Kansas, 1986).

10. Carry (or Carrie) A. Nation (1846–1911) was born Carry Amelia Moore in Kentucky. She married Charles Gloyd in 1867, to whose heavy drinking she attributed the ill health of their child, Charlien. Gloyd died six months after Carry left him. She married David Nation in 1877, following him to Kansas in 1889. There she campaigned against alcohol and tobacco. Clear in her religious mission, Nation began to agitate for enforcement of the 1880 prohibition of alcohol. She began to lead attacks on Kansas saloons in 1900. See Nation's 1905 autobiography, *The Use and Need of the Life of Carry A. Nation*, http://www.gutenberg.org/ebooks/1485, accessed May 4, 2020.

11. The infant mortality rate for Caucasians in the United States in 1880 was 35.2 per 1,000 live births. While "death rate" statistics make it difficult to calculate state-by-state figures in the 1880s, undoubtedly, the rate for babies on the frontier was significantly higher than for the country as a whole. The 2018 infant mortality rate for Kansas was 6.6 per 1,000 live births. The 2017 infant mortality rate in the United States was 5.8 per 1,000 live births. See https://www.cdc.gov/reproductivehealth/maternalinfanthealth/in fantmortality.htm, accessed May 4, 2020.

Chapter Two: The Town of Thayer

1. Thayer is approximately forty miles northeast of Longton.

2. The US-Mexican War, which began in 1846, ended in 1848.

3. The grasshopper (actually, the Rocky Mountain locust) invasion of 1874 began in Kansas in July and continued through August. Locust invasions continued to create havoc throughout Western states until 1877. After this invasions diminished, and the Rocky Mountain locust disappeared by the end of the century. (Locust invasions were replaced by grasshopper invasions.) The devastation in Kansas in the 1870s was extreme, as Bolinger relates, and led to widespread shortages of foodstuffs, especially corn. The effect of speculators buying and holding key grains, especially corn, in unaffected areas in states east of Kansas exacerbated the situation. In 1874 Kansas governor Thomas A. Osborne called a special session of the state legislature to deal with the emergency. State relief bonds were issued and local, county relief bonds were authorized. As Bolinger writes, additional relief, especially of non-foodstuffs, was provided by various donors from other states. See *New York Times*, August 17, 1874, 5; see also Jeffrey A. Lockwood, *Locust: The Devastating Rise and Mysterious Disappearance of the Insect that Shaped the American Frontier* (New York: Basic Books, 2005).

4. Nick Carter was a character in detective-story dime novels, first appearing in serial form in 1886 and in *The Nick Carter Library*, beginning in 1891. The character went on to have a career in radio dramas, films, television, and, later, novels. See Gary Hoppenstand, *The Dime Novel Detective* (Madison: University of Wisconsin Press/Popular Press, 1982), 182.

5. The Bender house, built in 1871, was approximately twelve miles from Thayer. See Edith C. Ross, "The Bloody Benders," *Collections of the Kansas State Historical Society*, vol. 17 (Topeka: Kansas State Historical Society, 1926–1928), 465.

6. The main road along which both locals and those headed further west traveled was located approximately one hundred yards from the Bender house. The nearest available water was three miles away, making the Bender house a convenient place for rest and refreshment. Travelers west often carried resources, usually in gold, which made them targets for thieves and bushwhackers.

The Bender house, described by Bolinger as a tavern, was described in later accounts as sixteen feet by twenty-five feet, with a sign over the front door reading "Groceries." In the back section, behind the curtain made from an old wagon cover, the Benders had installed a trap door under the stove. This led to a crude cellar, which had an outside door as well. Newly killed travelers were removed via the trap door and the cellar. The Bender daughter, Kate, claimed spiritualist powers and the ability to cure any disease for those who would stop at the house. Certainly, those who fell victim to the Bender trap no longer suffered from the disease that brought them into Kate's grasp.

The Benders fled in 1873 after the killing of the brother of a prominent member of the Kansas legislature inspired an investigation that led to the Bender house. Contemporary accounts of the fate of the Benders vary widely: some claim, as Bolinger writes, that a local posse captured and executed them. Others tell that the politician brother of the last victim led a predawn raid on the Bender house, killing the family and burying them. Still others reported seeing a family matching the description of the Benders board a train bound for Humboldt. See Ross, 464–479.

Chapter Three: Early Recollections

1. Or, ". . . snakes drawn"; the manuscript is unclear.

2. The American Broadcasting Company television series "Iron Horse" aired from 1966 to 1968. The setting for the series was the operation of the fictional "Buffalo Pass, Scalplock and Defiance Line Railroad" in the 1880s. See http://www.imdb.com/title/tt0059996/, accessed on May 4, 2020.

3. That is, fifty-eight to sixty inches tall at the withers. See chapter 1, note 3.

4. A filly is a young female horse. Technically, a colt is a young male horse, though Bolinger's use of the term to refer to young horses in general (the correct term is "foal") is a common error.

5. The "hard" or "long" winter of 1880–1881 was not the first difficult one for Kansas settlers. Several previous winters were characterized by severe, prolonged, or repeated blizzards of the type described by Bolinger, including the winters between 1870 and 1875. Numerous severe winters and blizzards followed in the 1880s and 1890s, with the blizzard of 1886 being of special note. See Craig Miner, *West of Wichita: Settling the High Plains of Kansas, 1865–1890* (Lawrence: University of Kansas Press, 1986), esp. 163–167; see also Jim Gray, *Desperate Seed*, 74, 75, 113–114, 158, 170–171.

Chapter Four: We Take a Journey

1. William Herbert Carruth (1859–1924) was born in Kansas. He received his undergraduate degree in modern languages at the University of Kansas in 1880, studied in Europe, and received the PhD degree from Harvard University in 1893. An accomplished linguist and poet, Carruth served on the faculty of modern languages and German at the University of Kansas

from 1887 to 1913, at which point he took up a position at Stanford University as professor of Comparative Literature and executive head of the English Department. The stanza quoted by Bolinger is from Carruth's poem and 1902 work of the same name, *Each in His Own Tongue and Other Poems*. Bolinger appears to be reciting the poem from memory. The actual, published text reads:

> A haze on the far horizon,
> The infinite, tender sky,
> The ripe, rich tint of the cornfields,
> And the wild geese sailing high,—
> And all over the upland and lowland
> The charm of the goldenrod,—
> Some of us call it Autumn,
> And others call it God.

Text from the 1906 edition (Chicago: P.F. Volland and Company). On Carruth, see the *William H. Carruth Collection* held by the Kenneth Spencer Research Library at the University of Kansas, including the Carruth biography at http://etext.ku.edu/view?docId=ksrlead/ksrl.ua.carruthwilliam.xml, accessed May 5, 2020.

2. Parsons is east of Longton and southeast of Thayer.

3. According to the Missouri Fox Trotting Horse Breed Association, the Missouri Fox Trotting Horse was developed from Arabian, Morgan, and plantation horses brought to the Ozarks region of Missouri in the early nineteenth century and later augmented by breeding with American Saddlebred, Tennessee Walking Horse, and Standardbred horses. As Bolinger indicates, the Fox Trotter was valued for its versatility and endurance but especially for its comfortable gait as a saddle or buggy horse. Contrary to Bolinger's concern, the Fox Trotter continues in popularity, being named the Missouri state horse in 2002. See https://mfthba.com/the-breed/history-of-the-breed/, accessed May 5, 2020.

4. The yellow Fish Brand slicker was a long oilcloth rain slicker coated with linseed oil, which had a distinct fish odor. Known as a "pommel slicker" that horse riders could wear with comfort in the saddle, the Fish Brand was developed and sold in 1881 by Abner J. Tower of Boston. More flexible and comfortable than the masticated India rubber and coal tar naphtha material developed by Charles MacIntosh in 1823 or the vulcanized rubber material that Charles Goodyear developed in 1839 and patented in 1844, the Fish Brand was highly desired, despite its odor. Modern replicas retain the name but not the odor. See Ronald R. Switzer, *The Steamboat* Bertrand *and Missouri River Commerce* (Norman: Arthur H. Clark Company/University of Oklahoma Press, 2013), 188.

Chapter Five: Fun on the Farm

1. The "two-pen dog trot" design is a log house—actually two log cabins joined by a common roof—that predates the Civil War. The sheltered area between the two cabins, the dog trot, provided shelter for dogs while keeping them close to the house, as Bolinger surmises. Three- and (rarely) four-pen houses were built by adding one or two ells or a "T" and extending the common roof. Architectural historians differ as to the origins of this style, with some pointing to Swedish and Finnish antecedents both in Europe and in eastern US settlements, while others contend that the British central-hall house construction common in some areas of the colonial and postcolonial Mid-Atlantic and South was an inspiration. Still others point to Alpine barn construction in German-speaking areas of Europe. Whatever the source or sources, this style and its variants were common in the mid and deep South and in the West from Texas northward in the nineteenth century. See Terry G. Jordan, *Texas Log Buildings: A Folk Architecture* (Austin, University of Texas Press, 1978; reissued 1994), 114–133.

2. That is, stone walls made by stacking stones without mortar to bind them.

Chapter Six: The Writing School

1. While various typewriter designs emerged in the early nineteenth century, commercially available typewriters began appearing in Europe and the United States in the 1870s. The Scholes and Glidden model introduced in 1873–1874 and produced by Remington featured the QWERTY or universal keyboard familiar to modern users and was an understroke or "blind" style of the kind described by Bolinger. Frontstroke or "visible" typewriters, where the typist could view his work without lifting the entire carriage, began to emerge in the 1890s. See Michael H. Adler, *Antique Typewriters: From Creed to QWERTY* (Atglen, PA: Schiffer, 2000).

2. Proverbs 22:1, "A good name is rather to be chosen than great riches; loving favor rather than silver and gold."

3. That is, the art or discipline of handwriting; penmanship.

4. The manuscript has "once."

5. While both young girls and young boys were dressed in pantalets prior to the Civil War, the use of pantalets for women and young girls remained popular through 1870 and diminished thereafter. Thus, Bolinger's comment that he believed the young girl he encountered in the 1880s was "the very last person in the United States or possibly the world to wear pantalets" is understandable. See Sara M. Harvey, "The Nineteenth Century," in *The*

Greenwood Encyclopedia of Clothing through World History, vol. 3, ed. Jill Condra (Westport, CT: Greenwood, 2007), 61.

Chapter Seven: New Scenes and Greener Pastures

1. The amendment was adopted in 1880; see chapter 1, note 8.

2. The Southern Kansas Academy was created and supported by the inhabitants of the Eureka area, under the control of the Southern Association of Congregational Churches of Kansas. Efforts began in 1884, and the school opened in 1886, in one brick building located on fifteen acres donated by residents. It offered several college preparatory courses of study, including the "classical," the "scientific," the "literary and normal," and a "preparatory" course "for those who do not see the need of a full college course." See anonymous compilers, *Columbian History of Education in Kansas* (Topeka, KS: Hamilton Printing Company, 1893), 141–142.

3. John A. Gregg was born in Eureka, KS, in 1877. He served in the Spanish-American War, following which he continued his education, graduating from the University of Kansas in 1902. He served in South Africa, returning to the United States in 1906, to serve in the African Methodist Episcopal (A.M.E.) Church. He was the pastor of a number of churches in Kansas and Missouri and was president of Edward Waters College in Florida and Wilberforce University in Ohio. After becoming a bishop in the A.M.E. Church in 1924, he was selected as the first African American president of Howard University, though he declined the appointment. During World War II, Gregg ministered to African American troops serving overseas on tours of the battle theaters, the second of which was at the request of President Roosevelt. Gregg is remembered today as one of the giants of the bishops of the A.M.E. Church. See Alexander Gregg, *First Bishop of Texas, By His Son, the Late Wilson Gregg, Edited and Extended by the Reverend Arthur Howard Noll* (Sewanee, TN: University Press, 1912), http://anglicanhistory.org/usa/agregg/no11912/07.html, accessed May 5, 2020; see also Kansas State Historical Society, "John A. Gregg," http://www.kshs.org/portraits/gregg_john.htm, accessed May 5, 2020.

4. It is important to keep in mind that this memoir was composed in 1967, at the height of the Civil Rights Movement and the attendant conflicts both in the South and in most major American urban centers.

5. That is, a worn-out, slow, or inferior horse.

6. Argifying is probably a misspelling of argufying, a colloquial term meaning "to argue, dispute, wrangle." See Angus Stevenson and Maurice Waite, ed., *Concise Oxford English Dictionary: Luxury Edition*, 12th ed. (Oxford: Oxford University Press, 2011), 69.

7. The manuscript has "grove."

8. A wood or metal worker's tool, consisting of a wooden handle and a metal blade, set at a right angle (90 degrees) to the handle. Also called a "tri-square."

9. That is, Hell. See chapter 1, note 5.

10. The earliest marriage statutes in Kansas, including the requirement that a marriage license be obtained, were enacted in 1867; see *Kansas Statutes (Annotated), Revised*, chap. 23 and especially article 1, originally §23-106 and since transferred to §23-2505, https://www.ksrevisor.org/statutes/chapters/ch23/023_025_0005.html, accessed May 5, 2020.

11. That is, the devil. Belial is sometimes used as synonymous with Satan. In 2 Corinthians 6:15, Belial (Greek: *Beliar*) is contrasted with Christ. The context, as made clear by 2 Corinthians 6:14, is a contrast of the light of Christ with demonic darkness. In the Hebrew Bible, "sons of Belial," as Bolinger uses it, refers collectively to wicked and abusive people. See Judges 19:22.

12. Railroad rights-of-way granted in the nineteenth century varied widely, but one hundred to two hundred feet from the tracks was common, with some extending beyond that. See Darwin P. Roberts, "The Legal History of Federally Granted Railroad Rights of Way," *Social Science Research Network*, July 9, 2008, http://papers.ssrn.com/so13/papers.cfm?abstract_id=1157498, accessed May 5, 2020.

13. For a discussion of the difficulties faced by farmers and the drop of farm prices in Kansas in the 1880s, see Introduction, pp. 7–8.

14. Hackney coaches or cabs were horse-drawn coaches for hire, the forerunner of the modern taxicab.

15. In the presidential campaign of 1888, Republican Benjamin Harrison (1833–1901) defeated incumbent Democrat Grover Cleveland (1837–1908). Cleveland won a majority of the popular vote, but Harrison won a decisive victory in the Electoral College. The campaign was noted for a lack of effort on Cleveland's part and for the exposure of corrupt campaign practices common to the era. In 1892, with Harrison lacking support from his own party and with economic problems increasing, Cleveland regained the presidency by defeating Harrison.

16. The Crystal Palace was built in London for the Great Exhibition of 1851. Championed by the Prince Consort Albert as a symbol of commitment to science and modern industry, the exhibition hall was an iron-framed building covered by more than one million square feet of glass, a considerable architectural and engineering feat for the time. Its exhibits highlighted industrial innovation and progress. Later moved to its own park at Sydenham Hill in South London, the Crystal Palace played an important role as a site in the early development of television. The hall itself was destroyed in a fire in 1936. See Peter Berlyn and Charles Fowler, *The Crystal Palace:*

Its Architectural History and Constructive Marvels (London: James Gilbert, 1851; repr., Boston: Adamant Media Corporation, 2005). As a symbol, the Crystal Palace was used by social theorists, novelists, and others in the later nineteenth and early twentieth centuries to both praise and condemn the effects and pretensions of industrial modernity and British imperialism.

17. The Quonset hut is a semicircular, prefabricated, all-purpose structure made from corrugated, galvanized metal. It is lightweight, inexpensive, and easy to assemble. Adopted by the US military early in World War II, the design originated in the World War I–era Nissen hut developed by the British. Many variations on the design were built during and after the war, and surplus huts became ubiquitous as temporary living and permanent storage buildings following the war. See Chris Chiei and Julie Decker, ed., *Quonset Hut: Metal Living for a Modern Age* (New York: Princeton Architectural, 2005).

18. Patrick S. Gilmore (1829–1892) was an Irish-born American bandleader and composer. After 1848, Gilmore led bands in the United States; he enlisted in the Union Army and eventually served as bandmaster general. He was one of the most important figures of American popular music in the second half of the nineteenth century, noted as the composer of the *22nd Regiment March*, the lyrics to *When Johnny Comes Marching Home*, and other popular tunes. Following the Civil War, Gilmore organized popular musical organizations and events in the Boston and New York areas and toured throughout the United States and Europe. He created the forerunners of Madison Square Garden and the Boston Pops music series. The March King, John Philip Sousa, was said to have regarded Gilmore as the Father of The American Band. See Frank J. Cipolla, "Patrick S. Gilmore: The Boston Years," *American Music* 6, no. 3 (Autumn 1988): 281–292; and https://www.songhall.org/profile/Patrick_S_Gilmore, accessed May 5, 2020.

19. A cutter is a type of horse-drawn sleigh.

20. A horse and carriage or buggy rented from a livery stable.

Chapter Eight: The Shape of Things in Little Things

1. That is, the Southern Kansas Academy in Eureka. See chapter 7, note 2.

2. Drover or cattle attendant laws originated in alarming loss rates for livestock, including cattle, in the early days of rail transportation. State laws regulating conditions for livestock began in Illinois in 1869 and spread to other states. Special cars, either "drovers' cars" or "drovers' cabooses" were built for the attendants. The combination of improved car designs, regular provision of food and water, and faster freight service helped reduce loss rates. See John H. White Jr., *The American Railroad Freight Car: From the*

Wood-Car Era to the Coming of Steel (Baltimore, MD: Johns Hopkins University Press, 1993), esp. 413, 430–431.

3. That is, Appaloosas, a breed of horse.

4. The modern Appaloosa is characterized by a spotted coat, especially on the hindquarters, as well as by some of the features described by Bolinger. While horses of this type appear around the world in representations stretching back to Paleolithic times, the American Appaloosa stems from the horses of the Nez Perce and Palouse Native American tribes, centered in the Palouse region of eastern Washington state and western Idaho. The Nez Perce acquired the horses by trade from the Shoshone and other tribes; the original source was Spanish horses, between 1700 and 1750. Careful breeding of the horses by the Nez Perce established what would come to be called "Appaloosas" as a source of great wealth and reputation; these horses drew the attention of Meriwether Lewis, who remarked upon them in February 1806 in terms not unlike Bolinger's. At the end of the brief, tragic struggle with the US Army known as the Nez Perce War, in October 1877, the Nez Perce horses that had survived were taken and sold to settlers. Thus, it is possible that Bolinger's horse came from the original Nez Perce stock. See the Appaloosa Museum, "History of the Appaloosa," http://www.appaloosamuseum.org/cms/default.asp?contentID=521, accessed August 13, 2009; see also Meriwether Lewis and William Clark, *The Journals of the Lewis and Clark Expedition*, vol. 6, ed. Gary E. Moulton (Lincoln: University of Nebraska Press, 1990), 312–316.

5. A phaeton is a small, light, horse-drawn carriage, without a coachman's seat and usually regarded as sporty. See chapter 11, p. 104; and http://www.georgianindex.net/horse_and_carriage/carriages.html, accessed August 13, 2009.

6. For a description of the Southern Kansas Academy, see chapter 7, note 2.

7. Joseph Whitefield Scroggs (1852–1940) was, in the words of one memorial notice, a "colorful figure" in the history of education in Kansas and Oklahoma. Born in Missouri, Scroggs received his undergraduate degree from Lafayette College (Pennsylvania) in 1875. After teaching in public schools in Missouri, in 1879 Scroggs became an educator in the Cherokee Nation Territory, in what became Oklahoma. An ordained minister, Scroggs founded a school, the Worchester (or Worcester) Academy, became pastor of a church, and founded and edited one of the first newspapers in the territory. He taught in Arkansas, where he was married for the first time, and farmed in Missouri. After his time at the Southern Kansas Academy (1898–1904) and after receiving an honorary Doctor of Divinity degree from Washburn College (1902), Scroggs returned to Oklahoma, where he taught at Kingfisher College (1904–1913) and received the MA degree from Lafayette (1910). In 1913, Scroggs joined the University of Oklahoma

and convinced the Oklahoma legislature to provide a $10,000 grant—an extraordinary sum at that time—to found one of the first university extension divisions in the country. He led this division until his retirement in 1927, after which he remained active in education and public service. Scroggs published a number of essays and bulletins, especially regarding debating; and, as Bolinger writes, he was a champion of music, compiling and publishing the *Songs of Lafayette*. See *Chronicles of Oklahoma* 20, no. 4 (December 1942): 427–428, http://digital.library.okstate.edu/chronicles/v020/v020p415.html, accessed August 14, 2009.

8. The manuscript reads "clientess."

9. "Wizard Oil" was a common term for alleged cure-alls sold by traveling patent medicine "doctors" in the nineteenth and early twentieth centuries. See, for example, the description of "Hamlin's Wizard Oil" from this 1905 advertisement in the Hopkinsville, KY, newspaper, the *Kentuckian*: "[Hamlin's Wizard Oil] is a treatment which affords a positive cure for rheumatism and allied diseases. Applied externally it relieves the pain at once. Taken internally, it cures permanently by purifying the blood of the lactic acid which causes the disease." *Hopkinsville Kentuckian*, Tuesday, February 28, 1905, 7, http://kdl.kyvl.org/cgi/t/text/pageviewer-idx?c=hopnews;cc=hopnews;q1=wizard%20oil;rgn=full%20text;idno=hop1905022801;didno=hop1905022801;view=pdf;seq=7;passterms=1, accessed August 16, 2009.

10. "The Arms of Tilly" refers to a Dutch family and company, Oliefabriek c. de Koning Tilly, founded in 1696 in Haarlem. The folk medicine they produced, *haarlemolie*, or Oil of Haarlem, was a mixture of sulfur, herbs—especially an extract of white mulberry—and terebinth oil (oil of turpentine), and was advertised as a general curative. Circa 1780, Nicolas de Koning Tilly, a descendant of the founder, published *The arms of Tilly: The virtues and effect of the remedy,[na]med Medicamentum Gratia Probatum id est [the remedy approved by grace].* (Haarlem, the Netherlands: John Enschied, 1780[?]). Bolinger appears to be reciting the motto adopted by de Koning Tilly from memory, though it is possible that Bolinger's version—"MEDICAMENTUM DEUS PROBATUM" (the remedy approved by God)—was a corruption of the original by the traveling salesmen he encountered. Haarlem Oil was manufactured by others outside of Haarlem, including in Germany, and its formula varied. See "Haarlem Oil," *The Pharmaceutical Era*, June 18, 1908, http://www.bottlebooks.com/questions/Oct2001/haarlem_oil.htm; on the pharmacochemical properties of Haarlem Oil, see Philippe Compain and Olivier R. Martin, *Iminosugars: From Synthesis to Therapeutic Applications* (Chichester, UK: John Wiley & Sons, 2007), 1, 296–297, 299.

11. That is, the use of Latin would be taken as demonstrating the truth of the claim.

12. "Stock fish" is a generic term describing dried fish, usually cod, that is stored in hanging groups or tied in bales. Traditional recipes for stock fish

occur in many European countries, from Italy to Scandinavia, but are especially common in Northern Europe. The Norwegian version described by Bolinger is lutefisk, dried cod treated with lye. While considered an acquired taste by many, lutefisk continues to be favored as a delicacy among descendants of Norwegian settlers in Minnesota and other parts of the northern plains, often in frozen form that simplifies preparation. For information and recipes, see The Sons of Norway, "Lutefisk," http://www.sofn.com/norwegian_culture/showRecipe.jsp?document=Lutefisk.html, accessed on August 16, 2009.

13. Bolinger's view of the situation prior to the Spanish-American War, and his account of the willingness of political parties and economic forces to engage Spain in war, and especially of the sinking of the *Maine* in Havana Harbor, is an accurate reflection of the views of much of America both at the time and for many years afterward. Historians are more suspicious on a number of counts. The causes of and willingness to engage in the war are complex matters, but for a number of years some historians have argued that the explosion of the *Maine*'s powder magazines that precipitated its sinking on February 15, 1898, was not caused by a Spanish mine, as claimed at the time, but was an accident caused by an explosion of coal dust in the bunkers adjacent to the powder magazines. The US Navy Board of Inquiry convened at the time concluded that a mine under the *Maine* had caused the explosion, a view that fed war fever in the United States. While the view that the Spanish were responsible for the sinking did not in itself cause the declaration of war by the United States, it did lead to a hardening of both the US and Spanish positions and contributed to pressure on President McKinley to take military action. See Hyman G. Rickover, *How the Maine Was Destroyed* (Annapolis, MD: Naval Institute Press, 1995 [originally published in 1976]); see also the Navy's current discussion of the issue, http://www.history.navy.mil/faqs/faq71-1.htm.

Late twentieth century American historians have argued that the economic and political domination of Cuba had long been a key goal of American foreign policy, a fact that effectively obscured and foiled the Cuban independence movement. See, for example, Louis A. Pérez, "The Meaning of the Maine: Causation and the Historiography of the Spanish-American War," *Pacific Historical Review* 58, no. 3 (1989): 293–322, and *The War of 1898: The United States and Cuba in History and Historiography* (Chapel Hill: University of North Carolina Press, 1998), and Walter LaFeber, *The Cambridge History of American Foreign Relations*, vol. 2. *The American Search for Opportunity, 1865–1913* (New York: Cambridge University Press, 1993), 129–159.

14. As noted in the text, Bolinger is referencing the first chorus of the popular song from 1898. The actual title is "My Sweetheart Went Down

with the Maine," attributed to Bert Morgan. A number of variations have been published. The chorus is very close to what Bolinger remembers:

> Chorus:
> Once I had a sweetheart, noble brave and true,
> Fearless as the sunrise. gentle as the dew.
> We had loved and waited, we had named the day,
> And we had pledged to wed each other in the month of May.

See http://www.musicanet.org/robokopp/usa/onceihas.htm, accessed August 16, 2009; see also Vance Randolph, ed., *Ozark Folksongs*, vol. 4. *Religious Songs and Other Items* (Columbia, MO: University of Missouri Press, 1980), 139.

15. That is, pledge of allegiance to the flag. The first "pledge to the flag," written by Francis Bellamy and published in 1892, was not a pledge to the flag of the United States but stated simply, "I pledge allegiance to my Flag and the Republic for which it stands, one nation, indivisible, with liberty and justice for all." It was a pledge that could be used by the citizens of any republic. The first state to require its recitation was New York in 1898, precisely in response to the declaration of war on Spain. The first pledge to the flag of the United States was created in 1923 and recognized by Congress in 1942. The clause, "under God," was added in 1954. See Peter Irons, *God on Trial* (New York: Viking Adult, 2007), 238–239; see also 4 *United States Code* Chapter 1, §4, http://uscode.house.gov/download/pls/04C1.txt, accessed August 16, 2009.

16. Widespread rumors of "embalmed" beef—including charges that the tinned beef issued to soldiers during the Spanish-American War was Civil War surplus—were the subject of investigation. The charge that formaldehyde was used in preserving the beef was rejected in an analysis conducted by the US Department of Agriculture's Bureau of Chemistry. See Ian MacLachlan, *Kill and Chill: Restructuring Canada's Beef Commodity Chain* (Toronto: University of Toronto Press, 2001), 154; see also Louise Carroll Wade, "The Problem with Classroom Use of Upton Sinclair's *The Jungle*," *American Studies* 32, no. 2 (Fall 1991): 86.

17. In 1898, Theodore Roosevelt (1858–1919) resigned as assistant secretary of the Navy to help organize and equip the First US Volunteer Cavalry, known as the Rough Riders. The action referred to by Bolinger took place on July 1, 1898, when then-Colonel Roosevelt led the Rough Riders and elements of other formations, including African Americans (so-called Buffalo Soldiers), in the capture of two hills, the second of which was San Juan Hill. The brief campaign of the Rough Riders, and especially the charge up San Juan Hill, has become a matter of highly contested legend. Roosevelt's troops did help carry the day, though Bolinger is correct that it was as part

of a larger force. For one version of the events of that day, see http://www.theodoreroosevelt.org/life/Rough_riders.htm, accessed May 6, 2020.

18. Congress declared war on Spain on April 25, 1898; US troops landed in Cuba on June 22; Spain surrendered Santiago, effectively ending the war, on July 17, with the Peace Protocol signed on August 12, 1898.

19. It is not clear whether Bolinger is being serious or ironic when he refers to the United States' enlightened treatment of the Philippines. After the Spanish surrendered at Santiago and for the next sixteen months while the permanent peace treaty was negotiated, Filipino insurgents who wanted independence contested the control of US occupation forces in the Philippines. In the final treaty, Spain ceded control of the Philippines to the United States in exchange for $20 million. In February 1899, full-scale war broke out between the insurgents and US occupation forces. The US strategy was to combine political pacification of the Philippines' propertied classes with military suppression of the rebels. US troops, frustrated by the guerrilla tactics of the insurgents, often resorted to torture of the enemy and attacks on civilians. The ultimate US victory was costly: 4,224 Americans died and 2,818 were wounded; 16,000 Filipinos were killed or wounded in military action. Estimates are that another hundred thousand or so civilians died from starvation and war-related calamities. See "The Spanish-American War and Its Aftermath," *Encyclopedia of the American Military*, 3 vols. (New York: Charles Scribner's Sons, 1994), reproduced in History Resource Center (Farmington Hills, MI: Gale), http://galenet.galegroup.com/servlet/History/, and "Spanish-American War," *Violence in America* (New York: Charles Scribner's Sons, 1999), reproduced in History Resource Center (Farmington Hills, MI: Gale), http://galenet.galegroup.com/servlet/History/, both accessed on May 6, 2020.

Late twentieth century historians have rejected earlier interpretations that US suppression of the Filipino revolution was rooted in a benevolent desire to improve life in the Philippines. In fact, Michael H. Hunt argues that by the 1890s, Americans saw the "perilous potential of revolution." By that he means that US leaders feared that Cuban and Filipino revolutionaries threatened US interests because their demands did not meet criteria the United States determined acceptable for revolution. Hunt says that an acceptable revolution created a minimum of disorder, safeguarded property rights (especially the property rights of US investors), and demanded moderate, constitutional political change. See Michael H. Hunt, *Ideology and U.S. Foreign Policy* (New Haven: Yale University Press, 1987), 18, 105.

20. Psalms 19:5.

21. When President William McKinley (1843–1901) was assassinated in 1901, Vice President Theodore Roosevelt succeeded to the presidency.

Elected in his own right in 1904, Roosevelt chose not to run in 1908, and William Howard Taft (1857–1930) served as the party's (and Roosevelt's) choice for president. Taft defeated William Jennings Bryan in 1908 but lost support after 1909 among Republicans in a series of policy and personal struggles between conservatives and Progressives, including Roosevelt.

Chapter Nine: Of Politics and Politicians

1. James A. Garfield (1831–1881) was the last US president to be born in a log cabin, and the second president (after Lincoln) to be assassinated, serving less than a year. Elected as a reformer, he attacked corruption within the executive branch and battled with the Senate during his brief tenure.

2. Chester A. Arthur (1829–1886) succeeded to the presidency upon Garfield's death in September 1881. Arthur supported the patronage system attacked by Garfield but championed civil service reform after becoming president. Tariff issues came to dominate presidential politics in the 1880s and continued into the 1890s, pitting Arthur against many southern and western interests.

3. Grover Cleveland was the first Democrat to be elected since James Buchanan in 1856. He was the only Democrat to serve as president from 1861 (with the inauguration of Republican Abraham Lincoln) to 1913 (with the inauguration of Democrat Woodrow Wilson).

4. For information on Cleveland and Harrison, see chapter 7, note 14.

5. Bolinger's observation that the 1890s were less than "gay" gives an accurate picture of the economic turmoil of the period. See the discussion of this period in the Introduction, pp. 10–11. William Hope "Coin" Harvey (1851–1936) was one of the popular figures who responded to the suspicion common among rural and western citizens that eastern and, to an extent, British financial interests were manipulating the economy to the detriment of the economically weaker areas outside of eastern cities. (City of London bankers exchanging their dollars for gold had played a major role in the economic collapse.) Harvey advocated bimetallism, with the free and vigorous use of silver as well as gold in monetary policy.

6. William Jennings Bryan (1860–1925), as Bolinger goes on to admit, was one of the finest orators of his era. An attorney and politician, Bryan, an advocate of free silver, allied himself with the Populist agenda and later ran for president as the candidate of the Populist Party. He opposed the high tariff and monetary policies that, in his view, championed the wealthy at the expense of the rural and poorer citizens. At the Democratic Convention of 1896, where he was nominated for the presidency, Bryan gave his famous "Cross of Gold" speech, declaring

If they dare to come out in the open field and defend the gold standard as a good thing, we will fight them to the uttermost. Having behind us the producing masses of this nation and the world, supported by the commercial interests, the laboring interests and the toilers everywhere, we will answer their demand for a gold standard by saying to them: You shall not press down upon the brow of labor this crown of thorns, you shall not crucify mankind upon a cross of gold.

William Jennings Bryan, "Address to the Democratic Convention," July 9, 1896. See *The Cross of Gold: Speech Delivered before the National Democratic Convention at Chicago, July 9, 1896* (Lincoln: University of Nebraska Press, 1996).

7. For a discussion of this conflict, see chapter 8, note 21.

8. George Frisbie Hoar (1826–1904), a Republican from Massachusetts, was elected to various state and national offices before being elected to the US Senate in 1877. He served until his death in 1904. See *Papers of George Frisbie Hoar*, Massachusetts Historical Society, https://www.masshist.org/collection-guides/view/fa0298, accessed May 7, 2020.

Chapter Ten: Opening the Indian Lands

1. The allotment system that Bolinger describes in this chapter was created by the Dawes Severalty Act of 1887 (also called the General Allotment Act). For a discussion of the Dawes Act and some of its consequences, see the Introduction, pp. 14–15 and notes 29–30.

2. While the Dawes Act required that individual allotments to Native Americans be held in trust for twenty-five years and prohibited sale or alienation of the allotments, by 1891 the act had been amended to allow for limited leasing to nonnatives. At first, allotments could be leased for farming or grazing for up to three years if the allotment holder was "disabled." In 1894 "disability" was joined by the much broader and more flexible concept of "inability" as grounds for lease, and the leasing period was extended to five years. In 1897 the 1894 revision was reversed in order to stem the tide of nonnative settlement. In all of these changes, the paternalistic approach to native land ownership, based on the notion of proven "competency," prevailed. The Burke Act of 1906 completed the cycle Bolinger describes by providing for the issuance of a certificate of competency or fee patent to Native American landowners prior to the end of the twenty-five-year period, thereby giving Native Americans the right to sell their land. The abuse of the system by nonnative land seekers was rampant. See Martha Royce Blaine, *Some Things Are Not Forgotten: A Pawnee Family Remembers* (Lincoln: University of Nebraska Press, 1997), 97–104.

3. In theory, Native Americans who held Dawes Act allotments that turned out to be the location of substantial oil deposits *could* (and sometimes did) become wealthy. In practice, those newly wealthy oilmen were usually brought under the supervision of the state or federal government for their own "protection," sometimes by state assignment to a generally corrupt guardianship program and sometimes by federal assignment to the status of "restricted" Indians (a legal quasi-incompetency). In one documented example, the result was that a Native American landowner, whose land was producing between $15,000 and $40,000 per month in oil royalties, received a small payment each month, while the Oklahoma state agents acting as guardians received four times as much for their duties. See Tanis C. Thorne, *The World's Richest Indian: The Scandal over Jackson Barnett's Oil Fortune* (New York: Oxford University Press, 2003); see also Ryan J. Carey, "Review of *The World's Richest Indian: The Scandal over Jackson Barnett's Oil Fortune*," *Business History Review* 79, no. 2 (Summer 2005): 376–379.

4. Bolinger appears to be reciting from memory. The actual phrase, "as long as the grass grows or the water runs," is from a letter to the Creek Indians from President Andrew Jackson upon their removal from Georgia, March 23, 1829; it promises a safe, secure, and permanent home in the trans-Mississippi. See Daniel E. Feller et al., ed., *The Papers of Andrew Jackson*, vol. 7, *1829* (Knoxville: University of Tennessee Press, 2007), 112–113.

5. That is, hawthorn.

6. For discussion of these "land rushes," see the Introduction, p. 15.

7. The Klondike gold rush of 1897 was as difficult and as bleak for most as Bolinger describes. The actual gold fields were in the Yukon Territory of Canada, not in Alaska. The common, though dangerous and extraordinarily difficult, route to the gold fields for many Americans was through American territory via the White Pass Trail, beginning at the port of Skagway, or via the Chilkoot Trail beginning at Dyea, over mountain passes to the Yukon River. For a contemporary account of the Klondike gold rush from a Kansas City newspaper, see "Gold Fever Raging," *Kansas City Journal*, July 27, 1897, p. 2, col. 3, https://chroniclingamerica.loc.gov/lccn/sn86063615/1897-07-20/ed-1/seq-2/, accessed May 7, 2020.

Chapter Eleven: Social Life in a Small Town

1. Girdling is a traditional method of killing a standing tree by encircling the trunk with a cut groove that interrupts the flow of sap between the roots and the crown. See US Department of Agriculture, Forestry Service, *Tree Girdling Tools*, 3, http://www.fs.fed.us/eng/pubs/pdfpubs/pdf99242809/pdf99242809pt01.pdf, accessed May 7, 2020.

2. The manuscript reads "twualy."

3. The Kerosene Circuit was a feature of small-town Kansas and Missouri life in the late nineteenth and early twentieth centuries. The phrase referred to small, low-budget touring companies staging productions in makeshift theaters with crude kerosene (or coal oil, as Bolinger describes them) lights. See James Fisher and Felicia Hardison Londré, *The Historical Dictionary of the American Theatre: Modernism*, 2nd ed. (Lanham, MD: Rowman & Littlefield, 2018), 371.

4. *Quo Vadis: A Tale of the Time of Nero*, is an historical novel by the Polish writer Henryk Sienkiewicz, published in Polish in 1896 (some editions have 1897) and in English translation in 1905. It was adapted for the English-speaking stage and premiered in Chicago in 1899. See "'QUO VADIS' ON THE STAGE.; Dramatization of Sienckiewicz's Novel Is Presented in Chicago," *New York Times*, December 13, 1899, 6. The title refers to the New Testament passage in John 13:36, where Simon Peter asks Jesus, "Lord, where are you going?" (In the Latin Vulgate, "Quo vadis?")

Bolinger's mention of "East Lynn" is a reference to a stage adaptation of the English novelist Ellen Wood's 1861 Victorian story, *East Lynne.*

5. That is, mixed gatherings of boys and girls.

6. A country dance for couples, of Celtic origins and later English development. See "Reels," *The Royal Scottish Country Dance Society*, https://www.rscds.org/learn/music-resources/types-tunes/reels, accessed May 7, 2020.

7. As Bolinger relates, a number of the fraternal and benevolent orders of that era organized around life insurance plans. For example, the Knights and Ladies of Security, founded in Topeka in 1892, expanded quickly in the northern plains states. By 1911, it had 120,000 members in thirty states. See *Kansas Historical Society*, https://www.kshs.org/kansapedia/security-benefit-association/15616, accessed May 7, 2020. Bolinger's reference to the Workmen is most likely to the Ancient Order of United Workmen, which, like the Knights of Pythias, organized after the Civil War in part as a cooperative insurance venture. Many of these groups had other functions in civic life, such as organizing community bands. See Albert A. Stevens, ed., *The Cyclopaedia of Fraternities* (New York: E.B. Treat and Company, 1907), 133, 131.

8. Anemonae (or anemone) are early spring to late spring flowering plants, the earliest of which herald the end of winter. As Bolinger recounts, the plants have been called "windflowers"; the name "anemone" comes from the Greek for "wind" (*Άνεμος*). See John Eastman, *The Book of Forest and Thicket: Trees, Shrubs, and Wildflowers of Eastern North America* (Mechanicsburg, PA: Stackpole Books, 1992), 1.

9. Southern Kansas Academy; see Introduction, pp. 12–13, and chapter 7, pp. 77–78 and notes 2 and 3.

10. Literally, "end of the century"; but often it has, as Bolinger uses it, specific reference to the cultural and artistic transformations that characterized the end of the nineteenth and beginning of the twentieth centuries.

11. For information on Washburn College (now Washburn University), see Introduction, pp. 12–13.

Chapter Twelve: Life in Topeka

1. The capital city Topeka is an excellent example of post–Civil War settlement trends in northeastern Kansas in the nineteenth century. According to the state census in 1865, Topeka had 958 residents, making it the sixth-largest city in the state. (Leavenworth was by far the largest settlement, with 15,409 residents.) While it suffered from the collapse of a land boom in the 1880s, by 1900, Topeka's population had recovered and stood at 33,608, with the total for Shawnee County at 53,727. See James R. Shortridge, *Peopling the Plains: Who Settled Frontier Kansas* (Lawrence: University of Kansas Press, 1995), 24; "Shawnee County," http://www.ksgenweb.org/shawnee/index.html, accessed May 11, 2020; "Topeka," in *Kansas: a cyclopedia of state history, embracing events, institutions, industries, counties, cities, towns, prominent persons, etc. . . . / with a supplementary volume devoted to selected personal history and reminiscence,* vol. 2 (Chicago: Standard Publishing Company, 1912), http://www.ksgenweb.org/archives/1912/t/topeka.html, accessed May 11, 2020.

2. The Smith Automobile Company was started in Topeka by Drs. Clement and Anton Smith in 1902 and continued production until 1911. As Bolinger notes, the Smith brothers manufactured trusses, but also artificial limbs, orthopedic equipment, archery gear, and harps. Their chief engineer, Terry Stafford, built his first automobile in 1900, and he and the Smiths are credited with building the first automobile production facility west of the Mississippi. The Great Smith model that was Bolinger's first car was one of three models built by the company, the other two being the Veracity and the Smith. In 1908, a Great Smith was the first automobile to drive to the top of Pike's Peak in Colorado. While its products were highly regarded, the Smith Automobile Company succumbed to competition from more cost-efficient models built by Ford and Olds. A well-equipped Great Smith in 1911, the last year of production, cost $2,787. In that year, Ford reduced the price of the Model T to $645 for the most inexpensive version. See *Kansas Historical Society*, "Great Smith Automobile," https://www.kshs.org/kansapedia/great-smith-automobile/10210, accessed May 11, 2020; "1911 Ford Model T Sales Leaflet," https://www

.thehenryford.org/collections-and-research/digital-collections/artifact/355527#slide=gs-320721, accessed May 11, 2020.

3. Ransom E. Olds (1864–1950) built his first, three-wheeled, steam-powered vehicle in 1887. He turned to gasoline-powered cars in the 1890s. Olds is credited with the development of the assembly line in 1901, when fire destroyed his Detroit factory and all of its machine tools, forcing him to rely on parts suppliers. That development and the switch to a smaller car reduced the price of the Oldsmobile from $2,382—a small fortune at the time—to just $625. The smaller Oldsmobile is often cited as the first commercially successful automobile in America. In 1904, Olds left the Olds Motor Works to create the REO Motor Company. See Frank B. Woodford and Arthur M. Woodford, *All Our Yesterdays: A Brief History of Detroit* (Detroit, MI: Wayne State University Press, 1969), 256–257.

4. The Stutz Bearcat was produced from 1912 to 1932 (a car was produced under that revived name, in very limited numbers, in the 1970s); the Maxwell ceased production in 1924 and the Maxwell Motor Company became the foundation of the Chrysler Corporation; the Packard ceased production in 1957. See Craig Cheetham, *Vintage Cars* (St. Paul, MN: Motorbooks, 2006), 172; and Evan P. Ide, *Packard Motor Car Company* (Charleston, SC: Arcadia, 2003).

5. These steam cars had ceased production by the 1920s.

6. The Elmore became part of General Motors in 1909 and ceased production in 1912. See http://www.remarkablecars.com/main/elmore/elmore.html, accessed May 11, 2020.

7. The Sears Roebuck Autobuggy, produced for Sears Roebuck by Lincoln Motor Car Works, was produced from 1905 to 1911. See https://www.hemmings.com/stories/article/sears-motor-buggy, accessed May 11, 2020.

8. For a discussion of railroad land grants and their role in Western plains settlement, see the Introduction, pp. 4–8.

9. Bolinger's account of the founding and evolution of Washburn College is accurate; see the Introduction, pp. 12–13.

10. William Asbury Harshbarger (1863[?]–1942) taught mathematics, biology, and botany at Washburn College. In addition to his teaching duties and gardening activities, he also organized and served as captain to a group of Washburn student volunteers during the Spanish-American War. See "Veterans Day Ceremony, Washburn University, Nov. 11, 2004," *Speaking of Kansas: Washburn Center for Kansas Studies*, November 2004, http://www.washburn.edu/reference/cks/newsltrs/F2004.html, accessed May 11, 2020.

11. Charlotte Mendell Leavitt (1867–1958) was professor of English and dean of women at Washburn College. See *Washburn College Bulletin 1917–1918*, 92, https://books.google.com/books?id=d7BGAQAAMAAJ&pg=PA92&lpg=PA92&dq=Charlotte+Mendell+Leavitt+Washburn&source=bl

&ots=KiXqsYn8MF&sig=ACfU3U110RqgJRbpmUkJuzoWo9Fv_h6rdg&hl=en&sa=X&ved=2ahUKEwjA68bGjazpAhXkUt8KHUuBAdIQ6AEwBXoECAkQAQ#v=onepage&q=Charlotte%20Mendell%20Leavitt%20Washburn&f=false, accessed May 11, 2020.

12. A breeches buoy—as the name implies—is a ring lifesaving buoy to which is attached a type of short canvas breeches or pants. The device is attached to a rope by means of a traveling block. In the era before air-sea rescue, the breeches buoy was used in a fairly complex form, including a Lyle Gun for launching the guide rope, for rescue of passengers and crews of ships that had run aground or were in danger of sinking near shore, especially when weather prevented the launching of rescue vessels. Breeches buoys were also used for ship-to-ship transfers. See "David Lyle," https://www.nps.gov/spar/learn/historyculture/david-lyle.htm, accessed May 11, 2020.

13. Charles M. Sheldon (1857–1946), an important leader in the Congregational Church and in the development of the Social Gospel movement in America, advocated what he termed "Christian Socialism." The social gospel sought to apply Christian principles to social problems, especially the problems created by industrialization. Proponents of the social gospel movement called on Christians to take an active role in addressing problems such as poverty and immorality. Christian Socialism sought to combine Christian ideals with Socialist political principles; Christian Socialists, however, distinguished their own views from those of Karl Marx. They advocated development of cooperative and communal economic ventures that were owned and operated in the interests of all as the best expression of Christian ideals. See Michael McGerr, *A Fierce Discontent: The Rise and Fall of the Progressive Movement in America* (New York: Oxford University Press, 2003), 66–68; Steven L. Piott, *American Reformers, 1870–1920: Progressives in Word and Deed* (New York: Rowman and Littlefield, 2006), 86–89; "Christian Socialism," *Encyclopedia of the American West*, 4 vols. (New York: Macmillan Reference USA, 1996). Sheldon edited the *Topeka Daily Capital* for a week in March 1900, following the theme that guided his sermons: "What would Jesus do?" During that week, circulation increased from 10,000 daily to 360,000 daily, forcing the paper to print many of the additional copies in other cities. See Young-Hoon Yoon, "What would Jesus do? Charles Sheldon's Legacy and American Evangelicalism" (PhD diss., Drew University, May 2006), https://search.proquest.com/openview/d344031e3b62be7c6d58605b5ca86b36/1?pq-origsite=gscholar&cbl=18750&diss=y, accessed May 11, 2020; see also "Worthy of restoration: Old Prairie Town continues effort to preserve the Rev. Charles Sheldon's legacy," *Topeka Capital-Journal On-Line*, https://www.cjonline.com/news/local/life/2017-08-25/worthy-restoration-old-prairie-town-continues-effort-preserve-rev-charles, accessed May 11, 2020.

14. For a discussion of Carry A. Nation and her role in the Kansas temperance movement, see the Introduction, pp. 13–14, and chapter 1, note 10.

15. Nation arrived in Topeka on January 26, 1901. She did not attack saloons immediately upon arrival, but one account indicates that "The wife of a joint-keeper hit Nation on the side of the head with a broom, knocking her bonnet off. It was reported that as Nation bent over to pick up the bonnet, the jointist's wife 'smote her upon that portion of the anatomy which chanced to be uppermost.'"

Nation continued her efforts in two stages, interrupted by travels outside the city. Her campaign was nonviolent for the first week. She spoke with saloon owners, attempting to convince them to close their businesses. Finding this ineffective, on February 5, 1901, Nation attacked; the so-called Home Defender units Bolinger describes were used, and the "Senate" saloon was smashed. A number of attacks followed, and Nation was arrested and released many times in Topeka. Eventually she was convicted and sentenced to twenty days in jail. She was assessed a fine of $100, plus $48.30 in court costs. In July 1901, Kansas governor William Stanley commuted her sentence. Nation's efforts in Topeka helped to initiate a second, revived stage of temperance enforcement in Kansas. See "Cool Things: Carry Nation's Hammer," *Kansas State Historical Society*, http://www.kshs.org/cool2/hammer.htm, accessed May 11, 2020; "Carry Amelia Nation Papers, 1870–1919," Manuscript Collection no. 744, *Kansas State Historical Society*, https://www.kshs.org/p/carry-amelia-nation-papers-1870-1919/15801, accessed May 11, 2020.

16. Despite the myth that Burnett's Mound would protect the city, the Fujita Scale F5 (the top of the scale) tornado that struck Topeka on June 8, 1966, caused enormous destruction to Washburn University and the rest of the city. Seventeen people were killed, and damage totaled more than $200 million, making it one of the most destructive tornados in US history. Washburn University alone suffered $10 million in damage. See "The 1966 Topeka Tornado," *United States National Weather Service*, https://www.weather.gov/top/1966TopekaTornado, accessed May 11, 2020.

Chapter Thirteen: The Era of Change

1. The manuscript reads "Lumas"; but, as subsequent references and the historical record show, the Union Pacific general counsel (and judge) in question was Nelson H. Loomis (1862–1933). See, e.g., *Union Pacific R. Co. v. Hadley,* 246 U.S. 330 (1918), where Nelson H. Loomis argued the case for the railroad.

2. Until 1897, these were the requirements for admission to the Bar in Kansas: proof that applicants had "read law for two years, the last of which

must be in the office of a regular practicing attorney"; testimony from the supervising attorney as to the qualifications and good moral character of the applicant; and that the applicant be both a US citizen and a resident of Kansas. Such qualifications entitled one to practice before district and inferior courts and, on motion, to practice in the state supreme court. See *Kansas General Statutes*, chap. 11, §2 (1868), as reprinted in *The General Statutes of Kansas*, compilation of 1876 (St. Louis, MO: W. J. Gilbert, 1876), 53–54.

Washburn University School of Law professor and former dean James J. Concannon, in his history of the Washburn School of Law, comments on the older practice of reading law and its use in Kansas: "Until 1903, applicants who satisfied any district court that they possessed the requisite learning were admitted to practice in all district and inferior courts, and then could be admitted upon motion to practice in the Supreme Court. The examinations administered by the district judges, or by committees of local lawyers appointed by them, often were oral and in many districts lacked rigor." James J. Concannon, "'The ideal place . . . for the establishment of a great Law School'—The Early Years of Washburn University School of Law," *Washburn Law Journal* 42:803–852, quote at 804.

3. Harvard law graduate Ernest B. Conant became the founding dean of the Washburn College School of Law at the age of thirty-three, serving from 1903 to 1907. The school began with forty-one students. See Washburn University School of Law, "History," http://washburnlaw.edu/aboutus/history.html, accessed May 14, 2020.

4. Henry F. Mason (1860–1927) served as a city attorney and state legislator in Kansas prior to his 1902 election to the Supreme Court of Kansas, where he remained until his death. Mason was awarded an honorary doctor of laws degree by Washburn College in 1919. See "County Seat Controversies in Southwestern Kansas," note 1, *Kansas Historical Quarterly* 2, no. 1 (February 1933): 45, http://www.kancoll.org/khq/1933/33_1_mason.htm, accessed May 14, 2020.

5. Dwight Bolinger (1907–1992), A. J. Bolinger's eldest son and the earliest recipient of a copy of the manuscript of this memoir, became one of the most important figures in linguistics in the twentieth century. He held a faculty position at Harvard in 1967, when this memoir was written. Dwight Bolinger received his undergraduate degree from Washburn College in 1930 and went on to receive the MA degree from the University of Kansas and the PhD from the University of Wisconsin, the latter in 1936. He held a number of teaching and research appointments, including Washburn College, the University of Southern California, Harvard University (professor of Romance Languages and Literature, 1963–1973; emeritus professor, 1973–1992), and Stanford University (visiting emeritus professor, 1978–1992).

6. Augustin Alba was one of the more colorful and controversial characters of Mexican origin in Topeka, and in Kansas more generally, in the first

two decades of the twentieth century. In addition to operating the restaurant that Bolinger refers to, Alba became a deputy sheriff or "special Mexican policeman" of Shawnee County. He was featured in a number of high-profile arrests, trials, and scandals, which highlight the troubled relationship between the Mexican and Anglo communities in Kansas in this era, the intragroup conflicts and rivalries within the Mexican community, and the tensions created by the revolutionary era in Mexico. As one example, Alba accused Dr. Pedro F. Osorio, the consul appointed by the Mexican Constitutionalist president General José Venustiano Carranza de la Garza, of organizing an extortion scheme for "protection money" among the Mexicans of Topeka. Osorio was the leader of the Mexican fraternal organization, the Unión Mexicana Benito Juarez (UMBJ); he had been appointed by Carranza to replace the former consul, who was deemed ineffective in promoting and protecting the rights of Mexican workers in Kansas. Osorio denied Alba's charge, claiming that Alba was using his position as an ally of Anglo law enforcement to promote political ends that favored his Anglo employers. See Michael M. Smith, "Mexicans in Kansas City: The First Generation, 1900–1920," *Perspectives in Mexican American Studies* 2, no. 32 (1989): 29–57; see also Teresa L. Torres, *The Paradox of Religious Latina Leadership in the Catholic Church: Las Guadalupanas of Kansas City* (New York: Palgrave MacMillan, 2013), especially chap. 1; and https://www.newspapers.com/clip/25878994/augustin-alba-hispanic-deputy/, accessed May 14, 2020; https://www.newspapers.com/clip/15172312/the-topeka-daily-capital/, accessed May 14, 2020; https://kansashistoricalopencontent.newspapers.com/clip/15175801/the-topeka-daily-capital/, accessed May 14, 2020.

7. Dean Christopher Columbus Langdell of the Harvard Law School replaced the Dwight Method of traditional lecture and drill with the Case Method (or Casebook Method) at Harvard in 1870. It was understandable that Dean Conant, a Harvard graduate, would bring that method with him to the new law school at Washburn. See David A. Garvin, "Making the Case: Professional Education for the World of Practice," *Harvard Magazine* (September-October 2003), http://harvardmagazine.com/2003/09/making-the-case.html, accessed May 14, 2020.

8. Literally, "father of the family"; traditionally, the male head of the household.

9. "Ll.B." (or, more commonly, LLB or LL.B.), is the abbreviation for the degree of Bachelor of Laws (Latin: *Legum Baccalaureus*). In modern American legal education—including at the contemporary Washburn University School of Law—the JD degree (Juris Doctor) is more common than the LLB.

10. Okmulgee is in east-central Oklahoma, due south of Tulsa.

11. Charles Curtis (1860–1936) was a prominent Topeka attorney and Republican politician. Like Bolinger, he was admitted to the Bar after reading law. Curtis read law with A. H. (Hib) Case, an attorney in Topeka. He

served in the US House of Representatives from 1892 to 1906. He left the House to complete an unexpired term in the Senate in 1907, where he served until he failed to be renominated in the primary of 1912. He regained a Senate seat in 1914. After failing to gain the presidential nomination in 1928, Curtis gained the vice presidential nomination on the successful Hoover ticket. While he appeared on the cover of *Time* magazine in 1932 and officially opened the 1932 Olympic Games in Los Angeles, the advent of the Great Depression doomed the Hoover-Curtis ticket in the election of 1932. Curtis returned to legal practice and died in 1936. His legacy as vice president is not a happy one: never a close confidant of Hoover, he was widely considered ineffective and was the model for the buffoonish vice president Alexander Throttlebottom in George and Ira Gershwin's 1932 hit *Of Thee I Sing*. "Curtis, Charles," in *Biographical Directory of the United States Congress*, http://bioguide.congress.gov/scripts/biodisplay.pl?index=C001008, accessed May 14, 2020; "Charles Curtis, 31st Vice President (1929–1933)," *United States Senate History*, https://www.senate.gov/about/officers-staff/vice-president/VP_Charles_Curtis.htm, accessed May 14, 2020.

12. The high opinion of Charles Curtis among some in the Native American areas of Oklahoma is unsurprising. While Curtis was a staunch, conservative Republican and was ridiculed as an ineffective vice president, he was the first person to reach such office who could trace his ancestry to a Native American tribe, the Kaw of Kansas. His mother was descended from the daughter of a Kaw chief and a French trader. As part of a treaty settlement, Curtis's grandmother received "Half-Breed Reservation No. 4," across the river from Topeka. Curtis spoke Kansa and French before he learned English and lived for a time with his grandparents on a reservation. Still listed on the tribal roll, Curtis was attentive to Native American issues throughout his life, even though a number of his actions—especially in his furthering of the allotment system—created more harm than benefit for Native Americans. See "Charles Curtis, 31st Vice President (1929–1933)," *United States Senate History*, https://www.senate.gov/about/officers-staff/vice-president/VP_Charles_Curtis.htm, accessed May 14, 2020.

13. For a discussion of the issues surrounding the attempt to create two states, see the Introduction, pp. 16–18.

Chapter Fourteen: The Birth of a New Commonwealth

1. While there were struggles between political parties over issues in the Indian and Oklahoma Territorial areas that would become Oklahoma in 1907, when Bolinger went to Weleetka, Republicans held power in Washington. Theodore Roosevelt was president. The Republicans held clear US House of Representative majorities in the Fifty-Eighth Congress

(1903–1905), increased that majority to nearly 2-to-1 in the Fifty-Ninth (1905–1907), and maintained a strong majority in the Sixtieth (1907–1909). These Republican House majorities were mirrored in the US Senate. See "Party Divisions of the House of Representatives (1789 to Present)," Office of the Clerk, US House of Representatives, https://history.house.gov/Institution/Party-Divisions/Party-Divisions/, accessed May 14, 2020; "Party Division in the Senate, 1789–Present," Senate Historical Office, http://www.senate.gov/pagelayout/history/one_item_and_teasers/partydiv.htm, accessed May 14, 2020; and http://www.archives.gov/legislative/features/oklahoma/, accessed May 14, 2020.

2. Barry M. Goldwater (1909–1998) served as senator from the state of Arizona from 1953 to 1965 and from 1968 to 1987. Goldwater was the unsuccessful Republican nominee for president in 1964, losing to Lyndon B. Johnson. Goldwater was known as a blunt-speaking, independent conservative who embodied Western conservative interests and values. In the early 1960s, his speeches included memorable, controversial lines, the best known of which came from his address to the Republican convention in 1964: "I would remind you that extremism in the defense of liberty is no vice, and let me remind you also that moderation in the pursuit of justice is no virtue." See "Barry M. Goldwater," http://bioguide.congress.gov/scripts/biodisplay.pl?index=g000267, accessed May 14, 2020; and Barry Goldwater, "Speech Accepting the Republican Presidential Nomination," delivered July 16, 1964, San Francisco, http://www.americanrhetoric.com/speeches/barrygoldwater1964rnc.htm, accessed May 14, 2020.

3. In 1875, Lydia Pinkham began marketing a patent medicine to ease menstrual pain. The effectiveness of its herbal component was no doubt augmented by its alcohol content of approximately 18 to 20 percent. Pinkham's remedy was an enormous commercial success, though that success was dampened when the company was forced to reveal the alcohol content by the Pure Food and Drug Act of 1906. Pinkham's Compound continues to be produced and marketed as an herbal and vitamin supplement, though without the alcohol. See Rebecca Rego Barry, "Was Lydia E. Pinkham the Queen of Quackery?" JSTOR Daily, November 22, 2017, https://daily.jstor.org/was-lydia-e-pinkham-the-queen-of-quackery/, accessed May 14, 2020; see also "Lydia Estes Pinkham (1819–1883)," http://ocp.hul.harvard.edu/ww/people_pinkham.html, accessed May 14, 2020.

4. That is, a .32-caliber handgun.

5. That is, the court upheld the original sale of the land.

6. Primitive Baptists separated from mainline Baptists in the mid-nineteenth century. Strict Calvinists, Primitive Baptists opposed an educated clergy and Sunday schools because these institutions did not exist in the New Testament. See William Glenn Jonas Jr., *The Baptist River: Essays on*

Many Tributaries of a Diverse Tradition (Macon, GA: Mercer University Press, 2006), esp. 2–5.

7. This application of many elements of Arkansas law to the newly created territory was an aspect of the Organic Act of May 2, 1890. See Jeffrey Burton, *Indian Territory and the United States, 1866–1906: Courts, Government, and the Movement for Oklahoma Statehood* (Norman: University of Oklahoma Press, 1997), 153.

Chapter Fifteen: Journey's End

1. Chalkley M. "Chalky" Beeson (1848–1912) had various occupations: he was a saloon keeper; sheriff—in which capacity, he and a US Marshal engaged in a shootout with a member of the Doolin-Dalton gang, leaving the bank robber dead in the streets; cattle rancher; farmer; violinist and organizer of the famous Dodge City "cowboy" band—which he conducted with a loaded six-gun; sometime posse member; actor in early Western films; and state legislator from Dodge City, Kansas. See "Chalkley M. Beeson," in William E. Connelley, *A Standard History of Kansas and Kansans* (Chicago: Lewis Publishing Company, 1918), http://www.ksgenweb.org/archives/1918ks/biob/beesoncm.html, accessed May 14, 2020; and Richard M. Patterson, *Historical Atlas of the Outlaw West* (Boulder, CO: Johnson, 1985), 140.

2. William Barclay "Bat" Masterson (1853–1921) was one of the most famous lawmen of the Old West. As Bolinger noted earlier, the legend and the reality of famous western lawmen often diverged, and that is the case with Masterson. Masterson and Wyatt Earp became "special policemen" in Dodge City in 1876, and the following year Masterson was elected sheriff. His term was marked by violence and political conflict. For most of the rest of the century, he traveled as a gambler, gunfighter and fight promoter, and occasional newspaper publisher. After the turn of the century, he moved to New York City and became a sportswriter and favorite of President Theodore Roosevelt. Masterson died in New York. See George Laughead Jr., "W. B. 'Bat' Masterson," *Ford County Historical Society*, http://www.kansashistory.us/fordco/batmasterson.html, accessed May 14, 2020.

3. James F. "Bud" Ledbetter (1852–1937) was a lawman in pre-statehood Oklahoma and in Kansas. He became famous for successfully fighting off a gang of train robbers in 1894 while serving as a guard on a Wells Fargo train running between Kansas and the Indian Territory. Like Beeson, he acted in an early Western film. See Glenn Shirley, *The Fourth Guardsman: James Franklin "Bud" Ledbetter (1852–1937)* (Waco, TX: Eakin, 1997).

4. William F. "Buffalo Bill" Cody (1846–1917) is to many the most famous, and to historians among the most controversial, of characters to

emerge from the Old West. Bolinger is unsparing in his contempt for Cody, a view shared by many over the years. Historians, after careful reconsideration of Cody's life, remain critical of his image and impact, but many have come to a more nuanced view of his historical significance. Cody was an early (1857) resident of Kansas, though he worked in a number of Plains States. Bolinger is correct that Cody acquired his nickname by killing large numbers of "buffalo" (bison) on contract with the railroads that were expanding in Kansas. (Cody was based in Ellsworth, Kansas, west of Bolinger's home area.) Cody served in the Union Army during the Civil War and as a scout with the Army's Fifth Cavalry after the war. As an Indian Scout, he engaged in a number of battles after 1868, for which he was awarded the Medal of Honor. (The medal was revoked in 1916 on the grounds that Cody was not a member of the regular armed forces; it was restored, posthumously, in 1989.)

Prior to 1872, Cody's life embodied both the "butcher" (of bison), as described by Bolinger, and aspects of the military adventurer that was celebrated and exaggerated in later years. After 1872, at the urging of dime novelist Ned Buntline, who had helped create the heroic "Buffalo Bill" image in the minds of easterners, Cody began another life as a showman, creating a burlesque of his own earlier exploits. Buntline had exaggerated or simply fabricated many of the accomplishments attributed to Cody, or had attributed to Cody the actions of others, including those of James Butler "Wild Bill" Hickock (1837–1876). The celebrity aspects of *Buffalo Bill's Wild West* show and its sequels drew Bolinger's special scorn. The many aspects of that celebrity are well beyond the scope of this note, but it is reasonable to say that Buffalo Bill Cody was a product of Bolinger's West and also a commercialized caricature of that West—both at the same time. See John Shelton Lawrence and Robert Jewett, *The Myth of the American Superhero* (Grand Rapids, MI: Wm. B. Eerdmans, 2002), 50–58; and "William Frederick Cody," *The William F. Cody Archive*, http://codyarchive.org/life/wfc.bio.00002.html, accessed May 14, 2020.

5. Charles Jesse "Buffalo" Jones (1844–1919) was born in Illinois and died in Topeka. His conversion from buffalo hunter to buffalo preserver was the subject of Zane Grey's *The Last of the Plainsmen* (New York: Grosset & Dunlap, 1908). In 1907, when Jones lived in Arizona near the North Rim of the Grand Canyon, Grey accompanied Jones on a nostalgic hunting trip in the desert that helped inspire Grey's telling of the Charley "Buffalo" Jones story. While Bolinger is correct in his description of Jones as trying to preserve the American Bison, Jones began that effort by cross-breeding bison and cattle in an effort to produce a hardier stock animal, which he called the "cattalo," one that could survive the brutal blizzards Kansas experienced in the 1880s. That effort was unsuccessful, largely because the resulting animal could not reproduce. Jones then turned to raising pure-bred

bison; this was more successful, but his herd did not exceed approximately 150 animals. While this was the largest herd in Kansas, it was only a part of the approximately 500 bison that remained in the United States in the 1890s. In addition to the Canadian herds Bolinger mentions, other, smaller herds were created in the United States beginning in approximately 1871. In the second decade of the twentieth century, programs to repopulate selected bison herds grew in the United States. In an ending reminiscent of Bolinger's own skepticism about the 1890s being described as "gay," Jones was forced by the hard financial times of the 1890s to sell his herd in order to pay his debts. In addition to Grey's book, see Kansas Historical Society, "Charles Jesse 'Buffalo' Jones," https://www.kshs.org/kansapedia/charles-jesse-buffalo-jones/12106, accessed May 14, 2020; and US Fish and Wildlife Service, "Time Line of the American Bison," https://www.fws.gov/bisonrange/timeline.htm, accessed May 14, 2020.

6. The line is from a popular 1884 Victorian tune, "Love's Old Sweet Song," lyric by G. Clifton Bingham, music by James L. Molloy. See "Love's Old Sweet Song," http://www.hyperion-records.co.uk/tw.asp?w=W4378, accessed May 14, 2020.